Mountain Biking in the
Yorkshire Dales

ABOUT THE AUTHOR

Hailing from the flatlands of Cheshire, the rolling fells and iconic limestone landscapes of the Yorkshire Dales have always held a special place in Ian Boydon's heart. He has been visiting the national park with a mountain bike for almost 20 years – starting as a teenager on a fully rigid Diamond Back. After graduating in History then training as a journalist, a reporting job on local newspaper *The Westmorland Gazette* enabled him to move northwards and have the Yorkshire Dales' trails within easy reach. This book is the culmination of years of exploring the national park's bridleways in search of the perfect ride. Now working in public relations, Ian still lives in the area and can be found riding his bike on his favourite routes in the Yorkshire Dales, and nearby Lake District, most weekends.

OTHER CICERONE GUIDES BY THE AUTHOR

Mountain Biking in the Lake District

Mountain Biking in the
Yorkshire Dales

by Ian Boydon

© Ian Boydon 2012
First edition 2012
ISBN 978 1 85284 676 3

Published by Cicerone
2 Police Square, Milnthorpe
Cumbria LA7 7PY
www.cicerone.co.uk

Printed in China on behalf of
Latitude Press Ltd.

A catalogue record for this book is
available from the British Library.
All photographs are by the author
unless otherwise stated.

Front cover: Riding among the limestone
on Great Asby Scar (Route 4)

Title page: It's a steep and loose pull out
of Kettlewell (Route 19)

Back cover: Following a track high above
Swaledale (Route 24)

SPECIAL THANKS

I would like to take this opportunity to
thank Kieran Kent, Frans Boydon, David
Mawdsley, Tony Finnen, Terry Makin,
John Melia, Stephen Macmillan, and
Ed Hill for their help in test riding the
routes in this book and also for their
time posing for photographs.

I would also like to say an extra
special thanks to my wife Nicola for
her continued support, her help with
photography and her understanding of
my passion for mountain biking.

ADVICE TO READERS

While every effort is made by our authors
to ensure the accuracy of guidebooks as
they go to print, changes can occur during the lifetime of an edition. If we know
of any, there will be an Updates tab on
this book's page on the Cicerone website
(www.cicerone.co.uk), so please check
before planning your trip. We also advise
that you check information about such
things as transport, accommodation and
shops locally. Even rights of way can be
altered over time. We are always grateful
for information about any discrepan-
cies between a guidebook and the facts
on the ground, sent by email to info@
cicerone.co.uk or by post to Cicerone,
2 Police Square, Milnthorpe LA7 7PY,
United Kingdom.

Contents

Medium loops

Long loops

Full day loops

Appendix

Symbols used on OS maps

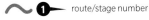 route/stage number

start/finish point

→ direction of main route

pub, café

For full OS symbols key see OS maps.

Difficulty grades

■ medium

▲ hard

◆ very hard

Emergencies

Always carry a charged mobile phone with you so that emergency services can be alerted in case of serious injury.

If you do need to report such an injury, first make note of all relevant details including location (giving the grid reference if possible), the nature of the injury and your mobile phone number. Then call 999 and ask for the police, then Mountain Rescue. Do not change your position until you are contacted by the rescue team.

The Mountain Rescue is a voluntary service manned by people who live in the region. They will send teams to find you on the fells if you are hurt. However, this service should not be used frivolously.

There are Accident and Emergency departments at Airedale General Hospital, in Steeton, near Keighley; Lancaster Royal Infirmary; Harrogate District Hospital; and Friarage Hospital, in Northallerton.

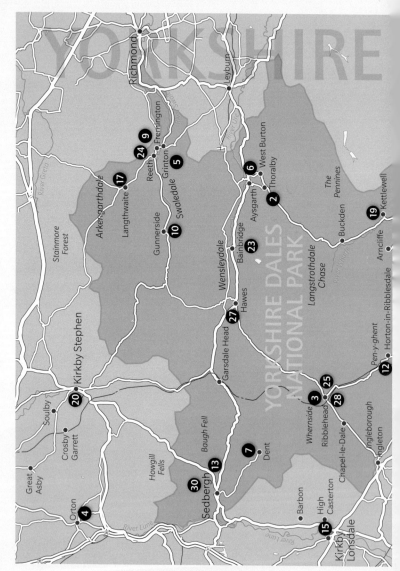

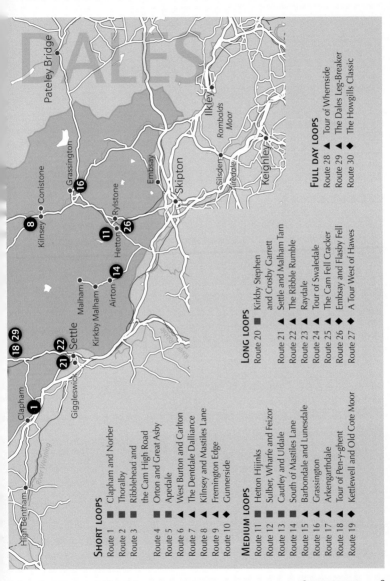

	Route	Title	% off road	Start/Finish	Distance
SHORT LOOPS	1	Clapham and Norber	95%	Clapham	14km (8¾ miles)
	2	Thoralby	85%	Thoralby	18km (11¼ miles)
	3	Ribblehead and the Cam High Road	75%	Ribblehead	18km (11¼ miles)
	4	Orton and Great Asby	55%	Orton	22.5km (14 miles)
	5	Apedale	80%	Reeth	23km (14¼ miles)
	6	West Burton and Carlton	90%	West Burton	15.25km (9½ miles)
	7	The Dentdale Dalliance	50%	Dent	19km (12 miles)
	8	Kilnsey and Mastiles Lane	80%	Kilnsey	19.25km (12 miles)
	9	Fremington Edge	70%	Fremington	21km (13 miles)
	10	Gunnerside	80%	Gunnerside	19km (12 miles)
MEDIUM LOOPS	11	Hetton Hijinks	80%	Hetton	25km (15½ miles)
	12	Sulber, Wharfe and Feizor	65%	Horton in Ribblesdale	26km (16¼ miles)
	13	Cautley and Uldale	60%	Sedbergh	28.5km (17¾ miles)
	14	South of Mastiles Lane	85%	Airton	29km (18 miles)
	15	Barbondale and Lunesdale	55%	Kirkby Lonsdale	25km (15½ miles)
	16	Grassington	75%	Grassington	27km (16¾ miles)
	17	Arkengarthdale	70%	Langthwaite	27km (16¾ miles)
	18	Tour of Pen-y-ghent	65%	Horton in Ribblesdale	28km (17½ miles)
	19	Kettlewell and Old Cote Moor	70%	Kettlewell	23km (14¼ miles)
LONG LOOPS	20	Kirkby Stephen and Crosby Garrett	55%	Kirkby Stephen	33km (20½ miles)
	21	Settle and Malham Tarn	80%	Settle	27km (16¾ miles)
	22	The Ribble Rumble	50%	Settle	32km (20 miles)
	23	Raydale	70%	Bainbridge	33km (20½ miles)
	24	Tour of Swaledale	80%	Reeth	33km (20½ miles)
	25	The Cam Fell Cracker	65%	Ribblehead	33.5km (20¾ miles)
	26	Embsay and Flasby Fell	60%	Hetton	30.5km (19 miles)
	27	A Tour West of Hawes	65%	Hawes	42km (26 miles)
DAYS	28	Tour of Whernside	70%	Ribblehead	39km (24¼ miles)
	29	The Dales Leg-Breaker	55%	Horton in Ribblesdale	58km (36 miles)
	30	The Howgills Classic	70%	Sedbergh	38.25km (23¾ miles)

GRADE	ASCENT	TIME	TIME OF YEAR	PAGE
■	380m (1250ft)	2hrs–3hrs	All year	29
■	480m (1575ft)	2hrs 30mins–3hrs	All year	33
■	500m (1640ft)	2hrs–2hrs 30mins	All year – good winter option	39
■	445m (1460ft)	3hrs–4hrs	All year – good winter option	45
■	730m (2395ft)	2hrs 30mins–3hrs	All year	51
▲	560m (1840ft)	2hrs 30mins–3hrs	Summer only	57
▲	710m (2330ft)	3hrs–3hrs 30mins	All year – better in summer	63
▲	595m (1950ft)	2hrs 30mins–3hrs	All year – good winter option	67
▲	700m (2300ft)	3hrs–3hrs 30mins	All year	73
◆	855m (2805ft)	3hrs–3hrs 30mins	All year	79
■	600m (1970ft)	3hrs–3hrs 30mins	All year – good winter option	87
■	550m (1805ft)	3hrs–4hrs	All year – good winter option	93
■	870m (2855ft)	3hrs–4hrs	All year – better in summer	99
■	790m (2590ft)	3hrs–4hrs	All year	105
▲	610m (2000ft)	3hrs–4hrs	All year	111
▲	740m (2430ft)	3hrs–4hrs	All year	117
▲	995m (3265ft)	4hrs–5hrs	All year	123
▲	690m (2265ft)	3hrs 30mins–4hrs	All year – better in summer	129
◆	1040m (3410ft)	4hrs–5hrs	Summer only	135
■	670m (2200ft)	3hrs 30mins–4hrs 30mins	All year	143
▲	700m (2300ft)	4hrs–5hrs	All year – good winter option	151
▲	955m (3135ft)	3hrs 30mins–4hrs 30mins	All year – good winter option	157
▲	1150m (3775ft)	4hrs–5hrs	All year	163
▲	1270m (4165ft)	4hrs–5hrs	All year – good winter option	169
▲	850m (2790ft)	4hrs–5hrs	All year	175
◆	850m (2790ft)	4hrs–5hrs	All year – better in summer	181
◆	1140m (3740ft)	4hrs 30mins–5hrs 30mins	All year – better in summer	187
▲	1095m (3595ft)	5hrs 30mins–6hrs	All year	197
▲	1280m (4200ft)	6hrs 30mins–7hrs 30mins	Summer only	205
◆	1260m (4135ft)	5hrs 30mins–6hrs 30mins	Summer only	213

The way to Calders (Route 30)

Introduction

Situated in the northern reaches of the Pennines, the Yorkshire Dales is England's second largest national park, after its near neighbour the Lake District. Despite being in close proximity to the Lakes, the Yorkshire Dales has an altogether different, more subtle character and a beauty that seems to grow with every visit. From a mountain biking point of view the riding is anything but subtle. A vast array of tracks and bridleways criss-cross the Dales – remnants from the region's history of lead mining and livestock droving, as well as Roman roads and other ancient byways. These trails provide vast scope for fat-tyre thrill-seekers.

Kilometres of fast-rolling lanes lined by picture-perfect dry-stone walls can be mixed with rocky drops down steep-sided gullies and sinuous tracks that meander over high deserted moorland. All this means that the Yorkshire Dales is a mountain biker's Shangri La waiting to be discovered.

There are no substantial areas of forestry in the Yorkshire Dales and therefore there are no purposely created trail centres. This matters little when the 'natural' riding is as plentiful and of such high quality as is found in this national park, providing a rich biking experience with stunning backdrops.

There are more than 20 dales within the Yorkshire Dales and their characters substantially vary, with dramatic limestone pavements found in the western dales, and old mining spoils found in northern and eastern areas. The good news is that the quality of the riding is superb in all areas of the Yorkshire Dales and the even spread of routes within this guide reflects this.

This book aims to guide you along the Dales' most thrilling trails while also avoiding

Start of the long plunge to Conistone (Route 16)

sustained sections of pushing and carrying. The few routes that do include significant pushes are clearly marked to forewarn you and have only been included because the rest of the ride is worth the effort.

Riders' abilities are different, and the days during the winter months are much shorter than in summer. For this reason care has been taken to include a good mix of routes of varying lengths and technical difficulty. This should ensure that the guide is enjoyed with confidence by mountain bikers of all levels of experience all year round.

So, what are you waiting for? Pick a route, saddle up and enjoy the ride.

GETTING TO THE YORKSHIRE DALES

Most people travelling to the Yorkshire Dales choose to go by car. For those travelling from the west the main access route is from the M6. Come off at J38 and take the A685 to get to Kirkby Stephen. For Sedbergh and Hawes exit at J37 and take the A684; and for Kirkby Lonsdale and Settle take the A65 from J36.

For those travelling from the east the main route to the Dales is the A1. For Swaledale exit near Richmond and take the A6108. For Wensleydale turn off onto the A684 and pass through Leyburn. And for the south Dales approach from Harrogate on the A59.

The only bus service able to carry bikes in the vicinity of the Yorkshire Dales is the Nidderdale Rambler, which operates on Sundays and bank holiday Mondays between Harrogate and upper Nidderdale.

National rail services operate on the Leeds to Morecambe line and the Leeds–Settle–Carlisle line. This famous line, which is considered one of Britain's most scenic, cuts through the heart of the Dales. With stations at Settle, Horton in Ribblesdale, Ribblehead, Dent, Garsdale and Kirkby Stephen, among others, the line can be used to easily reach the start of the following 11 routes in this book:

Route 3   Ribblehead and the
           Cam High Road
Route 7   The Dentdale Dalliance
Route 12   Sulber, Wharfe and Feizor
Route 18   Tour of Pen-y-ghent
Route 20   Kirkby Stephen and
           Crosby Garrett
Route 21   Settle and Malham Tarn
Route 22   The Ribble Rumble
Route 25   The Cam Fell Cracker
Route 27   A Tour West of Hawes
Route 28   Tour of Whernside
Route 29   The Dales Leg-Breaker

Please check with the relevant train company regarding bike access before travelling – normally two bikes are permitted on Settle to Carlisle trains.

ACCOMMODATION

There is an abundance of accommodation in the Yorkshire Dales, which can range from campsites, caravan parks, bed and breakfasts and hotels to the Dales Bike Centre in Reeth, which caters specifically for mountain bikers.

A good place to start your search for a place to stay is www.yorkshiredales andharrogate.com, the official tourism website.

EQUIPMENT

How much kit you decide to take along on a ride is up to you but there are certain items that should be con-sidered as essentials – and other bits that are going to make the experience much more enjoyable. Here is a run-down of the basic bits of kit required for mountain biking.

The Bike

There is a huge range of bikes on the market to choose from. Essentially you get what you pay for. Granted, not everyone is willing – or needs – to fork out thousands of pounds on a light-weight carbon fibre dream machine, but the real entry level for serious mountain bikes prob-ably comes in at around the £400 plus mark for a 'hardtail' – no rear suspension.

Full suspension bikes add more comfort and help with descending but you will be looking at paying more than £1,000 for a decent model.

Helmet

A helmet is an absolute essential. Anyone who considers it a good idea to go mountain biking without one probably has nothing to lose by risk-ing brain damage. Choose one that fits snugly and does not move around on bumps.

Full concentration being given on Asby Winderwath Common (Route 4)

Tools and spares

Mountain bikers should always be self-sufficient. If you run into difficul-ties out on the trail you have to rely on yourself to fix the problem. To do this you will need certain basic items:
- spare inner tubes – best taking at least two
- a mini-pump and/or CO_2 canisters
- a set of Allen keys and screwdrivers
- a set of tyre levers
- a chain tool and spare chain link
- a first aid kit

Hydration pack

There are a range of these on the mar-ket. Essentially they are rucksacks with a reservoir that allows you to drink on the move hands free, via a hose. These are strongly recommended as you can quench your thirst easily while still grinding up the climbs.

Gloves

These provide grip on the bars, warmth in winter and protection when you fall off (and you will fall off!).

Footwear

At the very least you will need a good sturdy pair of outdoor trekking or approach shoes (for grip and support). Clipless pedals and shoes with cleats are superb for giving you extra control – but only try these once you are confident on your bike.

Eyewear

Wearing eyewear is a personal choice. Many riders choose to wear sunglasses to reduce glare on bright days, but also to deflect mud and insects from their eyes on descents. A lot of riders, however, prefer to go without.

There is a large selection of glasses on the market with a variety of different coloured lenses, many of which are interchangeable depending on different light conditions.

Body armour

There has been a trend in recent years for increasing numbers of people to wear armour such as knee pads, elbow pads and shin guards to protect various parts of the body. These are also a personal choice. They may offer some peace of mind while descending; however, they can become quite cumbersome on the rest of the ride.

Other clothing

A breathable waterproof jacket is a must all year round. Even on dry, hot days you should pack one as the weather can change very quickly in hilly areas like the Yorkshire Dales.

Dropping into a gully near Carlton (Route 6)

Horton in Ribblesdale makes a good base for Dales biking

Other cycling-specific clothing like shorts with padding is essential and fast wicking jerseys will make you much more comfortable once you have got a sweat on.

Winter clothing

In winter you will want to wear more clothing to keep warm. A layering system is best, consisting of a base layer, thermal jersey and outer waterproof/windproof jacket. A layering system allows you to add or take off layers when necessary to regulate your temperature.

You need to take care of your extremities when the temperatures drop so thermal winter gloves are a must and you should also consider investing in a good pair of waterproof winter boots. Also a fleece-lined cap worn under the helmet is good for keeping the ears toasty.

Cycling-specific tights (worn under baggy shorts by the fashion conscious) are good at keeping you warm in winter. And a jacket made from a windproof fabric can also make a big difference by reducing the effects of wind-chill.

FOOD

It is vitally important that you take plenty of food with you on a ride. Mountain biking is a physically demanding activity and you should think of food as fuel. You will need to keep your energy levels topped up during the ride so take a selection of high carbohydrate foods such as energy/cereal bars, energy gels, sweets, sports drink and sandwiches.

The information box for each route in this guide contains information about where food can be bought along the way. However, many of the loops in this book take you out into remote areas far from shops and cafes so it is wise to pack sandwiches and other tasty items for these rides.

BIKE CHECKS

It is important to keep your bike properly maintained between rides to reduce the risk of mechanical failure when you are out having fun on the trails. Ensure that you wash your bike, degrease the chain and chainset and lubricate all moving parts. Before riding check your tyre pressures, as under-inflated tyres are more susceptible to pinch-flats (when the wheel rim cuts the inner tube). Also check your brake pads regularly to ensure there is sufficient wear left on them. It is also worth going round the bike occasionally to check that screws have not become loose.

WHEN TO RIDE

Mountain biking in the Yorkshire Dales brings different sets of challenges at different times of the year. During the summer the trail conditions will be at their finest. Hopefully they will be dry, and the weather will be generally good – most of the time. The main issue at this time of year can involve staying properly hydrated, so **remember to take sufficient liquids with you**.

Winter brings along different considerations. Although the limestone geology of the Dales drains well, the trail conditions can be wetter and muddier at this time of year. It is perhaps a wise decision to choose specialist mud tyres for the winter months.

The weather becomes a major consideration when choosing which route to ride in winter. Most of the rides in this book can be ridden at all times of the year. However, it is perhaps prudent to stay away from the higher levels if the weather is looking bad or if there is deep snow on higher ground. It is also worth remembering that the temperatures drop considerably, and the winds are stronger, when you are higher up.

In winter you should also remember that there are far fewer daylight hours in which to ride so choosing shorter routes is sensible. It can also be a good idea to include a light in your backpack if you feel you may be riding close to dusk – a puncture or a mechanical can easily cause delays and no-one wants to be stranded up on the moors in pitch darkness.

LIMESTONE

The Yorkshire Dales is famous for its unique limestone scenery and you will encounter significant amounts of this rock along the trails found on some of the routes in this book – particularly the routes in the south-west of the national park.

Dry limestone gives good and predictable grip, however it is worth noting that when wet limestone gives about as much grip as a slippery bar

Climbing above Sedbergh (Route 30)

Nice singletrack section on the bridleway into Uldale (Route 13)

of soap so take care where you place your wheels in rainy or wet conditions.

Rest and recovery

If you are planning a multi-day biking trip to the Yorkshire Dales remember your body needs time to rest and recover between rides. Choose rides of varying lengths on different days. After a big day in the saddle it is probably wise to do a shorter ride the following day. This should help ensure you have plenty in the tank for another long ride the day after.

You may want to try a recovery drink. These protein drinks, if consumed within an hour after finishing exercise, will help speed up your recovery and increase your ability to ride for longer the next day. There are plenty of specialist protein recovery drinks on the market but milk is a good, and cheaper, alternative.

Routes

The routes in this book are graded in relation to the technical difficulty of the terrain they pass across.

The grading system is as follows:

■ medium
▲ hard
◆ very hard

Even attempting the blue routes will require competent bike handling skills and a degree of confidence in your abilities.

Those new to the sport should attempt the blue routes first before progressing onto the more challenging red and black routes. Once you have a few of these under your belt your technique should steadily improve.

The abbreviations used in the route descriptions are as follows:

Abbreviations and symbols used in the route descriptions

← left
→ right
↑ straight ahead

N north
S south
E east
W west

NW etc   northwest etc
LH and **RH** left-hand and right-hand

- Easy to miss paths to look out for when en route are noted in **bold green**; warnings of steep, dangerous or possibly crowded routes in **bold red**.

- Place names in route descriptions that appear on their maps are noted in **bold**.

- Roads are shown as `A683`.

- Grid references are shown as SD 745 692.

- Important signs along the way are noted in *red italics* in route descriptions.

Maps

This book includes extracts from 1:50,000 Ordnance Survey maps to help ease your navigation of the routes. The descriptions have sufficient detail to be used alone but the maps are to be used in conjunction with them to help you to stay on the right track. In addition, the following Ordnance Survey 1:25,000 Explorer maps are recommended for the routes in this guide:

- **OL2** The Yorkshire Dales Southern and Western areas
- **OL19** Howgill Fells and Upper Eden Valley
- **OL30** Yorkshire Dales Northern and Central areas

Timings

Each route description has an estimated time for how long it should take to get around. These timings are a rough guide and the actual time will vary depending on fitness and experience, time of year, weather conditions, and possible punctures or mechanical problems, as well as pub or café stops and the time taken to appreciate, and perhaps photograph, all the magnificent views on offer throughout the national park.

Riding time

Times have been provided as a rough guide for each route. The following is a general rule of thumb:

- **Short loops**
  2hrs–3hrs 30mins
- **Medium length routes**
  3hrs–5hrs
- **Long routes**
  4hrs–6hrs
- **Full day routes**
  more than 6hrs

Rights of way

Mountain bikers are allowed to use bridleways, permitted bridleways, green lanes, BOATs (Byways Open to all Traffic) and some white roads. Riding on footpaths is not permitted and great care has been taken to avoid footpaths in this book. If you find you have ventured onto a footpath during a ride then it is highly likely that you have taken a wrong turn. In this case you are advised to retrace your steps and try to find the correct bridleway (very occasionally footpath signs are incorrectly put up on bridleways, but this is rare).

A minority of mountain bikers deliberately venture onto footpaths. However, this practice should be frowned upon as it damages the reputation of the majority who ride within the access rules. When out on a bike you are an ambassador for the sport and your actions reflect on mountain biking as a whole.

Finally, always give way to other path users, including walkers and horse riders. When passing others smile, say hello and remember to thank people who move to let you through.

Erosion

The erosion of paths within the national park is an ongoing problem, however the Yorkshire Dales National Park Authority has made significant improvements to many bridleways that were horrendous quagmires only a few years ago. A ban on 4x4 vehicles on certain byways has also helped matters.

Try to keep your impact on the landscape to a minimum by not skidding (this is a sign of lack of control more than anything), keeping to the centre of paths and riding through puddles rather than skirting round them, which only serves to widen puddles and muddy areas.

TRAIL CENTRES

There are no purpose-built trail centres within the Yorkshire Dales. The nearest is at the Forestry Commission's estate at Gisburn Forest, south of Settle just over the border in neighbouring Lancashire. Given the lack of a significant Forestry Commission estate within the Yorkshire Dales this situation is unlikely to change in the near future.

Crossing the narrow stone bridge near Wharfe (Route 12)

The dirty dozen

The following is a list of 12 of the best descents in the Yorkshire Dales. However, there are plenty more within this book that made it a tough choice.

1 **Stake Road (Route 2 Thoralby)**
A long fast blast from the heights of Stake Allotments back into the quiet village of Thoralby. There is nothing technical here, just high speed fun.

2 **Descent to Cote (Route 6 West Burton and Carlton)**
Big and varied, this superb descent has a bit of everything. Fast as well as rocky and technical, the views on a clear day add to the drama of this spectacular plunge.

3 **Flintersgill (Route 7 The Dentdale Dalliance)**
This technical delight becomes increasingly steep, rocky and sketchy the closer it gets to Dent. A cracking descent that rewards the brave.

4 **Mastiles Lane into Kilnsey (Route 8 Kilnsey and Mastiles Lane)**
This classic Dales descent starts off rocky and loose before opening out into a freakishly fast blast down the eastern flank of this ancient byway.

5 **Storthwaite (Route 9 Fremington Edge; Route 16 Arkengarthdale)**
This long twisting descent starts as a sublime piece of singletrack that opens out to give a fast weaving drop to Storthwaite Hall.

6 **Barbondale from Bullpot Farm (Route 15 Barbondale and Lunesdale)**
A varied plunge that becomes trickier near the bottom providing an excellent drop into the steep-sided Barbondale.

7 **Scot Gate Lane (Route 16 Grassington)**
A huge descent over a variety of terrain. The views are as excellent as the riding on this drop down Wharfedale's eastern flank to Conistone.

8 **Hull Pot to Horton in Ribblesdale (Route 18 Tour of Pen-y-ghent)**
This fast blast down a wide walled track with occasional rocky moments is great fun, however take care as this path is very popular with walkers.

9 **Old Cote Moor to Litton (Route 19 Kettlewell and Old Cote Moor)**
Initially very technical, this massive drop into Littondale then becomes increasingly speedy as it opens out over grassy pasture before giving a fitting finale above Litton itself.

10 **Embsay Crag (Route 26 Embsay Crag and Flasby Fell)**
Very steep tricky singletrack takes you from the summit of Embsay Crag while its lower slopes allow for more pace along the twisting bridleway.

11 **Craven Way into Deepdale (Route 28 Tour of Whernside)**
This excellent descent of a walled lane is rocky and rutted. Watch out for the drainage channels and the sketchy left-hander.

12 **Bowderdale from The Calf (Route 30 The Howgills Classic)**
This steep, rocky descent into Bowderdale leads to an amazing stretch of singletrack. This cracker is about balance and picking the line of least resistance.

Pre-ride checklist

There is nothing worse than driving to the start of your planned route for the day only to discover you have forgotten an essential piece of equipment like your helmet or clipless shoes.

Here is a checklist of essential items to tick off when getting your gear ready the night before:

- Bike
- Helmet
- Shoes
- Clothes
- Gloves
- Hydration pack
- Waterproof jacket/trousers
- Food
- Drinks
- Map
- Guidebook
- First Aid kit
- Spare tubes/puncture repair kit
- Pump
- Mini tool set
- Change of clothes and towel
- Cash
- Mobile phone

On the excellent rollercoaster descent towards Newby Head (Route 25)

The wide gravel-surfaced track past the old mine works beside Old Gang Beck (Route 10)

SHORT LOOPS

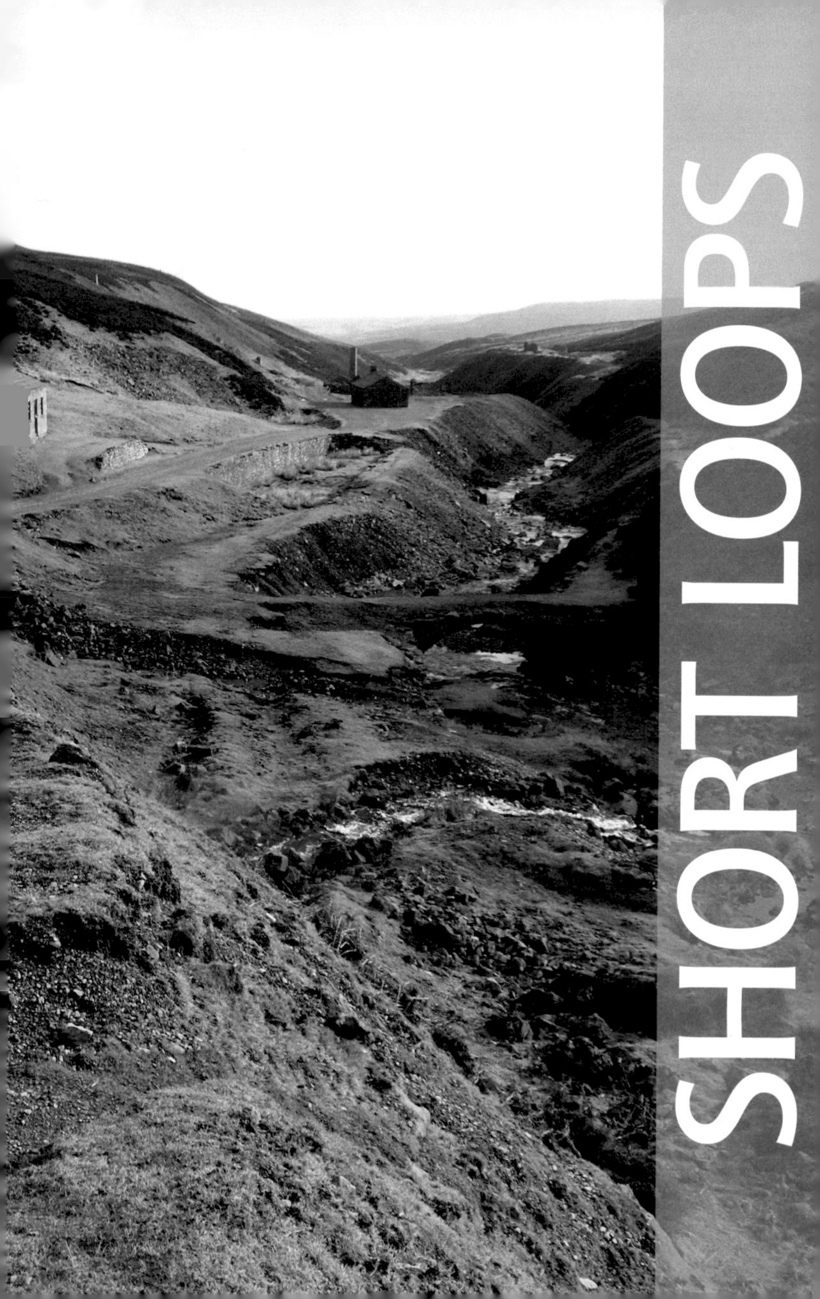

The fun grassy descent from Long Scar

1 Clapham and Norber

Start/Finish	Clapham SD 745 692
Distance	14km (8¾ miles)
Off road	13km (8¼ miles)
On road	1km (½ mile)
Ascent	380m (1250ft)
Grade	■
Time	2hrs–3hrs
Parking	Pay and display in Clapham
Pub	New Inn, Clapham
Café	Reading Room Café Bar, Clapham

Clapham is an unspoilt Dales village nestling in the south of the national park. It makes an excellent base for a short mountain biking loop that takes in the enjoyable lanes and bridleways that surround the small fell of Norber. A highlight of this route is riding through the atmospheric tunnels by the church in Clapham – plunging into the darkness is particularly interesting on the return trip.

Overview

Clapham is left by passing the church and riding through two dark tunnels on a stone-surfaced bridleway. This gives a good challenge but is never too steep and should be conquered without problem by the relatively fit. A left turn takes you on to the Long Lane track, which is a steady pull onto the higher ground below Thwaite Scars. The route's highest point is soon reached and is swiftly followed by a nice fast blast on a smooth grassy trail. Good singletrack takes you

into the peaceful hamlet of Wharfe and is followed by a couple of sections of easy walled bridleways.

The return leg is via a climb of Thwaite Lane, which brings you to the final cracking drop back into Clapham along the same trail on which the route began. Watch for the drainage ruts and the darkness of the tunnels on this fast plunge.

DIRECTIONS

1 Turn → out of the pay and display car park in **Clapham** and follow the lane to meet the church. Turn → by a millennium stone and ride towards a gate under a stone archway. Before reaching the gate turn ← onto a bridleway signed to *Austwick*. Climb through tunnels and up the wide walled lane to meet a junction.

2 Turn ←, signed *Pennine Bridleway Selside*, and descend briefly before riding gradually upwards along stone-surfaced Long Lane. Keep to the walled lane until it culminates at a gate opening out into a field. Pass through and bear → to continue climbing on the now grassy bridleway.

3 Pass through another gate, below a rocky outcrop, and continue rising. The trail bears **left** and then forks. Take the **LH** option and follow it as it bends around the side of **Long Scar** hill. This path soon meets another fork by an expanse of limestone pavement. Bear ← then, within a short distance, turn → onto a narrow distinct grassy bridleway marked by a small stone cairn.

4 Descend this excellent trail. Part way down the path forks – bear ← to follow the more distinct option. At the bottom bear → and ride to a gate and go through. Continue descending a wide stone-surfaced track until meeting a fork on the ←. Take this walled lane signed to *Wharfe* and follow to meet a stone bridge over a stream. Cross this and continue along the bridleway, which soon narrows to singletrack and gives a cracking short drop into **Wharfe**.

Entering the dark tunnels of Clapham

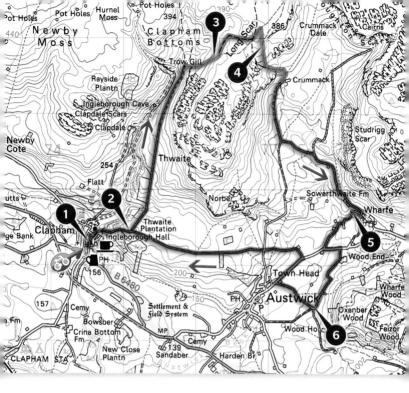

5 Turn → in the hamlet and follow the unsigned bridleway ↑ to leave Wharfe. At the end of this enjoyable singletrack path turn ← onto a tarmac lane at Mill Bridge, ride a short distance and then turn first → onto a bridleway signed to *Feizor*. Bear → at the cottage and keep on this walled lane until meeting a junction of five trails. Turn → to take the path signed *Pennine Bridleway Austwick*.

6 A short descent takes you to another stone bridge. Cross this and keep riding to pop out on the tarmac lane again. Turn → and ride ahead until meeting a turn ← signed *Pennine Bridleway Thwaite Lane*. Climb this wide walled track to meet a crossroads and continue ↑ following the sign to *Clapham*. Keep riding ↑ along Thwaite Lane as it rises then levels out, before leading to a fast bumpy drop back into **Clapham** and through the tunnels you passed through at the start of the ride.

Starting the excellent descent off Stake Allotments

2 Thoralby

START/FINISH	Thoralby SD 999 867
DISTANCE	18km (11¼ miles)
OFF ROAD	15km (9¼ miles)
ON ROAD	3km (2 miles)
ASCENT	480m (1575ft)
GRADE	■
TIME	2hrs 30mins–3hrs
PARKING	Behind the village hall
PUB	The George Inn, Thoralby
CAFÉ	Bring sandwiches

85% OFF ROAD

The little-known village of Thoralby lies on the corner of Bishopdale and the much larger Wensleydale. It is also situated at the bottom of a storming mountain biking descent. It might not be a technical rock fest, however the wide and firm surface of the walled bridleway descent of Stake Road and Haw Lane means it can be ridden as fast as you like. The rest of the ride is essentially gradual climbing over interesting terrain, to lead you to the long final plunge back into Thoralby.

OVERVIEW

A steep pull out of Thoralby is followed by easy riding over an undulating bridleway to reach a tarmac lane. A short pedal into Thornton Rust leads to steady ascending on a narrow track over moorland. On reaching Carpley Green the climbing steepens a little on a wide loose stone byway to the high ground of Stake Allotments. At the top of this track a left turn takes you onto the long bridleway descent of Stake Road back to Thoralby, which more than makes up for the climbing in the first half of the ride.

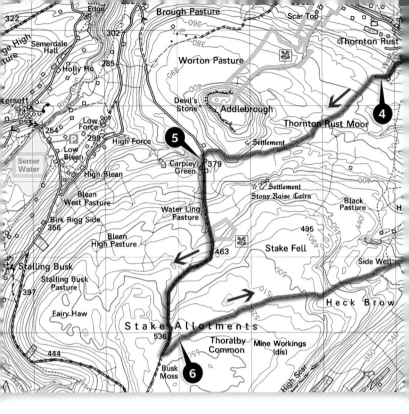

Directions

1 Head **SE** through **Thoralby** climbing gradually to meet a turning on the **right** with a large tree on the corner. Take this to pass between cottages and climb steeply on a loose rocky bridleway. Climb to meet a gate on a **LH** bend. Turn → to pass through the gate, which is signed as a bridleway, and continue climbing very steeply for a short distance to meet another gate.

2 Pass through the gate and into the grassy field beyond. **The track is vague here** but head towards the far **RH** corner of the field to reach a gate near a large oak tree. Pass through the gate following the bridleway sign. The track drops steeply to meet a gate and a ford. Cross this and continue on

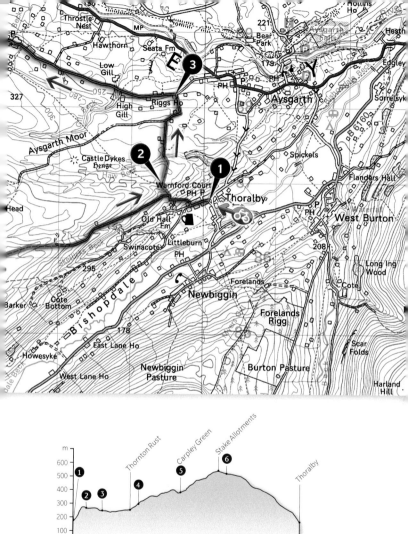

the walled lane ahead. At a fork with a footpath fingerpost sign bear → and follow the track to meet a tarmac lane.

❸ Turn ← and follow the road into the village of **Thornton Rust**. Turn ← to take the lane opposite the Village Institute building, following a sign for *car parking*. At the small car park fork ← after a shallow ford and follow the good track as it climbs steadily onto moorland.

❹ Bear ← at the fork with a fingerpost. Enjoy good moor riding on the undulating grassy path, passing through the first gate and continuing ↑. Keep to the obvious track and pass through a gate with a stile. Continue ↑, bearing ← at a fork, ignoring the permissive footpath to the right, and pass through a gate signed bridleway. With Addlebrough hill on the right, the bridleway eventually gives a short singletrack descent to emerge on tarmac at **Carpley Green**.

Approaching Carpley Green

5 Turn ← and continue ↑ through the farm taking the wide loose rocky Busk Lane track as it climbs up onto **Stake Allotments**. When the path plateaus at the top look for a bridleway sign on the **left** to *Thoralby*. Turn to follow this vague trail, which is initially singletrack. Head towards the stone cairn and pass just to the **right** of it.

6 The track now becomes wider. Follow it to a gate and pass through. Continue ↑ ignoring a left fork and later a right turning. Eventually the path begins to descend. As it drops to meet a wider track by a bridleway sign bear ← to continue descending. Pass through a shallow beck and continue ↑ to meet a signed fork of bridleways. Continue ↑ on the main trail, called Stake Road, and follow it as it passes over grassy fields. The bridleway soon emerges onto a firm wide walled track that gives an exhilarating fast drop all the way back into the centre of **Thoralby**. Turn ← in the village to return to your starting point.

Riding the twisting trail towards Whernside

3 Ribblehead and the Cam High Road

START/FINISH	Ribblehead SD 765 793
DISTANCE	18km (11¼ miles)
OFF ROAD	13.5km (8½ miles)
ON ROAD	4.5km (2¾ miles)
ASCENT	500m (1640ft)
GRADE	■
TIME	2hrs–2hrs 30mins
PARKING	Lay-by at Ribblehead
PUB	The Station Inn, Ribblehead
CAFÉ	Bring sandwiches

75%
OFF ROAD

Deep within the Yorkshire Dales, on the high fells between Hawes and Ingleton, is the source of the River Ribble. The Ribble begins its long journey to the sea beyond Preston after starting as a trickle at Ribblehead. This area is made famous by the formidable towering viaduct that carries on its back the Settle to Carlisle railway – lauded as one of the most scenic rail journeys in Britain. Mountain bikers can also enjoy a pretty spectacular short tour of this area by climbing north-east from Ribblehead, and by making use of a track recently upgraded to bridleway status that provides a fast and fun return leg. This route is largely free of significant technical difficulty and is a good scenic introduction to riding in this part of the Dales.

OVERVIEW

A short ride along the B6255 towards Hawes takes you to the first off-road section – an initially tarmac surfaced bridleway that soon becomes grassy and climbs steadily over Gayle Moor. The gradient soon relents to provide interesting riding on a now undulating and rock-strewn bridleway. A short tarmac spin then takes you to Newby Head Pass and the start of another bridleway. This wide track climbs steadily again, providing splendid views on clear days, and whisks you to a tarmac section of the former Roman road – the Cam High Road. A right turn here and the off-road track soon reappears to give a very long, fast and highly enjoyable – albeit gate-punctured – descent back to the B6255 just above Ribblehead. A short

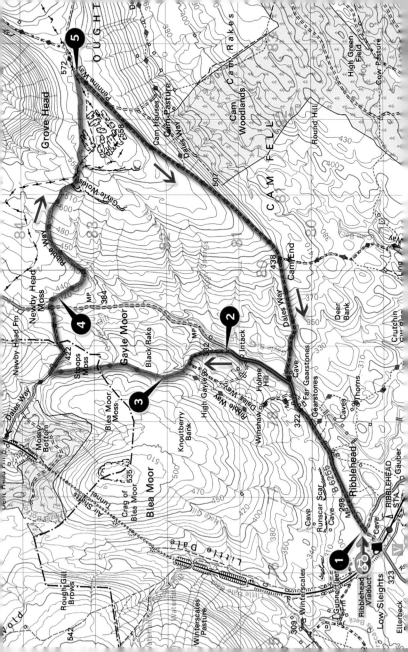

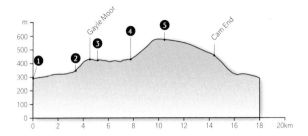

retracing of your tracks earlier in the day returns you to the start point overlooking the impressive viaduct.

DIRECTIONS

1 Starting at the road junction by the magnificent **Ribblehead Viaduct**, head **NE** along the `B6255` towards Hawes, climbing steadily. Pass a footpath turning on your left and also ignore a wide track forking off to the right before reaching a bridleway turning **left** signed *Dent Head*.

2 Take this and climb the tarmac lane, crossing a cattle grid, to reach a bend by a wall. Continue ↑, signed bridleway, onto a grassy track. Keep climbing to meet a gate. Pass through and follow the main track, ignoring two turnings on the left.

3 This good path soon flattens and gives enjoyable riding across **Gayle Moor** before ending at a tarmac lane high above Dentdale. Turn → and ride to a T-junction at Newby Head Pass. Turn → then immediately ← through a gate and onto a bridleway.

4 Climb this very good track as it meanders over moorland to meet a gate below a small rock escarpment (look behind on a clear day for a cracking view of the distant Lakeland fells). Pass through the gate and stay on the distinct trail as it becomes grassy. Eventually you will meet a gate in the drystone wall on your **right**.

Descending the Cam High Road

5 Pass through the gate and emerge at a tarmac lane by gates to Cam Farm. Turn → and pass through Cam Farm gate. Follow the tarmac lane to meet a fork on a sharp **LH** bend – take the → fork to continue ↑ onto the stone-surfaced Cam High Road. Follow this wide track, which after a short distance gives a very long and fast blast down towards Ingleborough. Pass through two gates, ignoring a footpath turning at a large cairn, and meet a fork on **Cam End** as Ribblehead Viaduct comes back into view. Bear → and continue the cracking descent back to meet the B6255. Turn ← and retrace your steps back to the start.

Enjoying the return descent of the Cam High Road

Crossing a beck just outside Orton

4 Orton and Great Asby

START/FINISH	Orton NY 622 082
DISTANCE	22.5km (14 miles)
OFF ROAD	12km (7½ miles)
ON ROAD	10.5km (6½ miles)
ASCENT	445m (1460ft)
GRADE	■
TIME	3hrs–4hrs
PARKING	Free parking in Orton
PUB	George Hotel, Orton
CAFÉ	Orton Chocolate Factory Shop and Coffee House

55% OFF ROAD

The Orton Fells contain the largest expanse of limestone pavement outside the Ingleborough area and this spectacular landscape, which lies just north-west of the Yorkshire Dales, is considered worthy for inclusion in the national park as part of expansion proposals. This route provides a fine tour through this beautiful landscape. Although lacking in significant technical difficulty, the ride contains plenty of stunning views and fun trails. This is a good ride to build the confidence of less experienced riders.

OVERVIEW
Starting from Orton the initial stages consist of easy riding alongside a gently flowing brook before bringing you to a steep climb up Orton Scar. A short blast on tarmac is followed by a section on wide track before a fun descent on a singletrack grassy bridleway.

Another short section of road is followed by more grassy riding, a wooded track and then a long descent to the hamlet of Drybeck – watch your speed near the bottom. You then ride along tranquil back lanes to the sleepy village of Great Asby. A climb out of the village on road leads to a great track that winds up onto Asby Winderwath Common and among the limestone pavements. A fun grassy descent down the other side and then it is a short ride along a quiet road back into Orton.

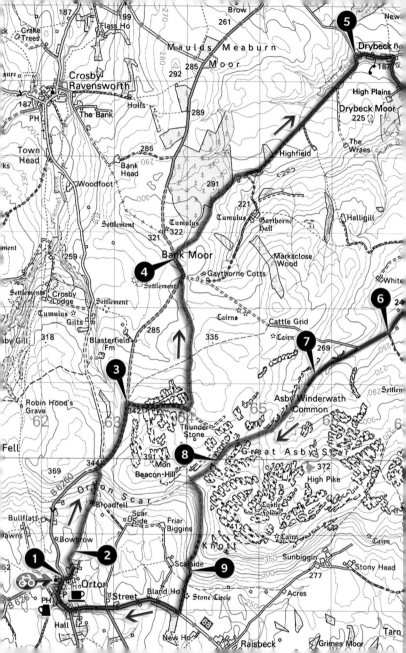

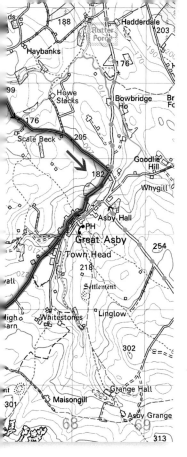

Directions

1 From the centre of **Orton** take the `B6260` N for a very short distance. Before leaving the village turn first → onto a side street, then before meeting a stone bridge over a brook, turn first ←. Follow the brook upstream to meet a sign (easy to miss) for a bridleway pointing ← between houses. Follow the sign and at the rear of the houses continue along the singletrack bridleway to meet a field.

2 Continue ↑ through fields alongside the babbling brook, passing through several gates, to reach a farm. Go through the farmyard and continue ↑ to climb steeply on a grassy track up **Orton Scar**. Pass an old kiln and rejoin the `B6260`. Turn → and descend to meet an obvious track on the **right** (just after a lay-by and shortly before a bridleway fingerpost).

3 Ride along the wide track to meet a signed crossroads with a bridleway. Turn ← and descend a fun grassy singletrack bridleway. Continue ↑ at a crossroads of paths to join the `B6260` again at a junction. Continue ↑ on the road to meet a bridleway sign on the right.

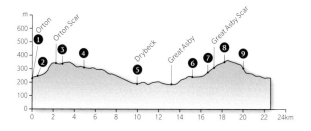

Ignore this sign (which is in the wrong place) and continue a short distance to meet a wide grass track on the **right** marked with two large rocks and near a *sheep hazard* road sign.

4 Take this and descend a short distance to a gate. Pass through and go ↑ over a grassy pasture to meet another gate at some woodland. Follow this sometimes muddy trail to a farm building. Fork ←, keeping to the higher path as it becomes a walled track, and pass through another gate. Descend the partially surfaced track over a field to meet a gate. Pass through and onto a long straight lane, the surface of which changes from stone to tarmac part way down. Continue descending ↑ until reaching a T-junction on a bend at the bottom.

5 Turn →, pass through the hamlet of **Drybeck**, and turn next →. Follow this undulating lane for around 2.5km to meet a crossroads. Turn →, pass through the idyllic village of **Great Asby**, and continue along the main lane as it climbs out the other side.

6 Ignore the first bridleway turning on the left and continue to where the road bends sharp **right** at a fork with a bridleway. Continue ↑ here turning onto a wide stone-surfaced bridleway signed *Copper Mine Lane*. Follow this firm track as it climbs onto **Great Asby Scar**.

7 After passing through a gate continue ↑ to the next gate. Pass through this then look for a gate in the wall on your **right** with an information sign. Go through this and follow the obvious singletrack bridleway as it skirts beneath the large limestone pavement. The path soon cuts between slabs of limestone and meanders its way to meet a fork with a sign. Bear ← and climb to meet a gate with another large information sign.

Passing limestone near Great Asby

The fun return descent off Orton Scar

8 Pass through the gate and ride ↑ to meet a junction with a fingerpost. Turn ← here, passing through a gate, and follow the obvious bridleway as it bends around the curve of the fellside above the drystone walls and drops at speed to eventually meet a gate.

9 Go through and descend the Knots Lane byway to meet a T-junction with a tarmac road. Turn → and follow the road back into **Orton**. Turn → at the T-junction at the end to ride back into the village centre.

Climbing onto Harkerside Moor

5 Apedale

START/FINISH	Reeth SE 038 993
DISTANCE	23km (14¼ miles)
OFF ROAD	18.5km (11½ miles)
ON ROAD	4.5km (2¾ miles)
ASCENT	730m (2395ft)
GRADE	■
TIME	2hrs 30mins–3hrs
PARKING	In the centre of Reeth
PUB	The Bridge, Grinton
CAFÉ	Dales Bike Centre, Fremington

Apedale is a high valley perched between the much larger Swaledale and Wensleydale. Like much of the northern Dales it has been scarred by old mining activity. This route, starting in Reeth, provides a fun and scenic tour south of Swaledale and through the deserted and atmospheric Apedale. Although the first half of the ride is a bit of a slog with seemingly continuous climbing, the second half rewards your hard labour with a string of cracking descents. Firstly the long plunge into Apedale and the fast track to Dent Houses. Then further blasts from the top of Greets Hill, and lastly the drop to Cogden Hall, ensure you arrive back in Reeth smiling.

OVERVIEW

A long steep tarmac climb from Grinton Bridge takes you to the start of your off-road adventure. Don't rest easy however, as there is more climbing still ahead. The wide track on Harkerside Moor seems to wind continuously upwards, although after a while it does undulate to give some respite. One last climb up Whitaside Moor takes you to the head of Apedale from where a cracking descent shoots you into the belly of this high valley. A ride along a fast trail takes you to a crossroads of tracks and the start of a climb onto Greets Hill. From the cairn-strewn summit an interesting path weaves down to meet a tarmac lane. A short, fast, drop down here and you reach another bridleway. Ride along this grassy path to meet another road and climb to reach the final off-road section – a long, speedy and,

5 APEDALE 51

at times, slippery plunge down to Cogden Hall. From here a short tarmac spin returns you to Reeth.

DIRECTIONS

1 Descend from the centre of **Reeth** along the `B6270` to **Grinton**. After crossing the River Swale turn immediately → (in effect ↑) and climb through the village. Keep climbing to meet a fork on the **right** signed to *Redmire*. Take this lane, riding past bridleway turnings on both sides, to meet a **LH** bend. Turn → onto a signed bridleway forking from this bend.

2 Ride along this grassy and stony path to meet a more distinct track. Bear → (in effect ↑) and follow this good, wide track as it climbs high then undulates above Swaledale for 6km. Keep going ↑ as the obvious trail passes a large dark wooden building, ignoring all turnings. Eventually you reach a bridleway T-junction by a pile of rubble on **Whitaside Moor**. Turn ← and continue climbing steadily to meet a gate.

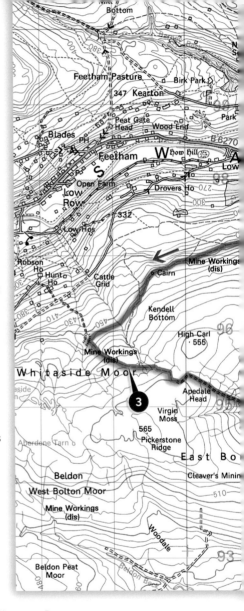

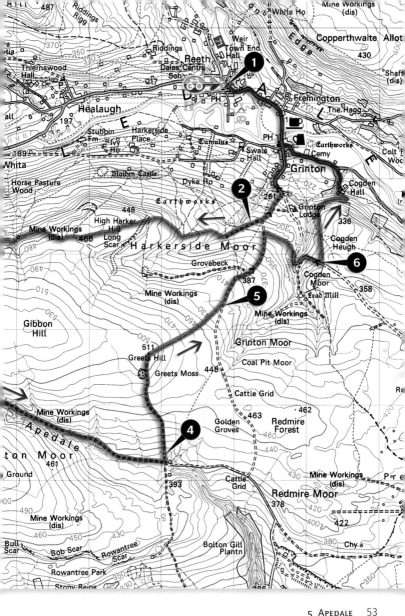

Dropping down the loose track at Apedale Head

3 Pass through the gate and enjoy a good, fast descent into **Apedale**, with a steep and rocky sting in its tail. As the track levels continue riding ↑. Ignore a fork to the left and keep to the main path as it takes you to a crossroads by buildings at Dent's Houses.

4 Turn ← and climb the wide track directly to the cairns at the summit of **Greets Hill**. Pass through the gate and take the path running alongside the wire fence on your left. Keep to this track as it widens and begins descending – there are a multitude of lines to choose from. Keep descending roughly ↑ to meet a tarmac lane and turn ←.

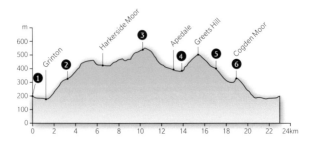

5 Descend the lane, ignoring the first bridleway turning on the left, and turn → at a crossroads of signed bridleways. Ride along the grass-surfaced bridleway, which undulates before dropping to meet another lane. Turn → and follow the road as it dips slightly before climbing steeply up **Cogden Moor**. Ride to meet a signed bridleway at a gate on the **left**.

6 Pass through the gate and descend the grassy bridleway to meet another gate. Continue ↑, keeping to the main track as it swings **right**, and enjoy a fast blast to the farm at **Cogden Hall**. Continue riding to meet a tarmac road and turn ←. Follow this road to pass through Grinton and return to the start in **Reeth**.

Fun riding on the Apedale Road

Negotiating a water obstacle en route to Carlton

6 West Burton and Carlton

START/FINISH	West Burton SE 017 866
DISTANCE	15.25km (9½ miles)
OFF ROAD	13.75km (8½ miles)
ON ROAD	1.5km (1 mile)
ASCENT	560m (1840ft)
GRADE	▲
TIME	2hrs 30mins–3hrs
PARKING	On street in West Burton
PUB	Fox and Hounds, West Burton
CAFÉ	Village Tea Shop, West Burton

90% OFF ROAD

The village of West Burton nestles in the north-east of the national park and is a real hidden gem for those that discover it. West Burton is also the starting point for a cracking little mountain bike ride around the fells to the east of the village. This loop utilises some fine tracks that link West Burton to Carlton village providing good riding, great views and one of the best descents in the whole of the Yorkshire Dales. The final drop on the return leg from Carlton is an absolute joy – steep, very long, full of rocks and obstacles, as well as fast grassy sections and magnificent vistas. It never fails to please.

OVERVIEW

A stiff but manageable climb up Morpeth Gate will soon have you in the red zone, though cracking views down Wensleydale will take your mind off some of the suffering. This is followed by a wide fast track to a road and more steep climbing. A long byway descent, punctuated by the occasional gate, then whisks you to Carlton. The return journey is made by a long

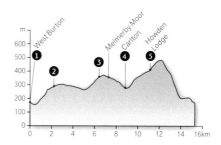

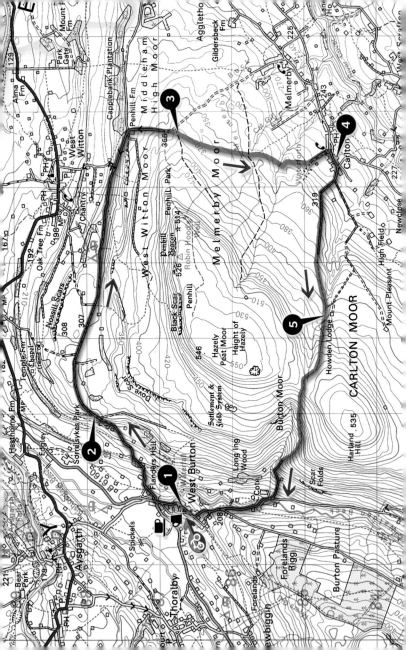

Enjoying the fast track over Melmerby Moor

climb onto the shoulder of Harland Hill and Height of Hazely. The descent from here is truly superb and will have you grinning all the way back to West Burton.

DIRECTIONS

❶ From the centre of picturesque **West Burton** head downhill (**N**) to meet a T-junction and turn ➔ (in effect ⬆). Take the first turn ➔ (signed *weak bridge*), cross the stone bridge over Walden Beck and follow this lane as it deteriorates into a stone and mud surfaced byway. The track soon gives a long, and sometimes steep, climb out of the valley along Morpeth Gate. Ride to a junction with a footpath at a fingerpost and bear ⬅ to stay on the byway.

❷ Ride along this wide and fast byway, High Lane, until it culminates at a tarmac lane. Bear ➔ and climb the aptly named Witton Steeps. Ignore a left turn and continue climbing along the tarmac lane – passing a bridleway on the right – to reach a cattle grid. Cross this and turn immediately ➔ onto a byway, marked by a *no motor vehicles* sign.

❸ The grassy track climbs for a short distance before levelling and then giving a good, long descent on an obvious path that cuts across open ground on **Melmerby Moor**. Follow this, ignoring all turnings, to meet a gate. Pass through and, when the track forks at a corner of the drystone wall on your **left**, bear ➔ (in effect ⬆). Follow this now less distinct track across the next few fields – passing through a couple of gates. After crossing a steep-sided beck go through a gate next to a derelict stone barn. Take the obvious path, which starts next to the wall on your **left**, and descend to another gate. Keep to the main track as it eventually drops you into **Carlton** to meet a T-junction. Turn ➔.

4 Ride to meet a junction on a **LH** bend – still in the village – and turn ➔ (in effect ⬆). Ride along this lane to meet a junction by a fingerpost. Both directions are signed *West Burton*, and the tracks do converge higher up the fell, however the better option is ➔. Take this stone-surfaced walled bridleway as it climbs steadily to reach a large stone building – **Howden Lodge**. Just before reaching the lodge's gate the track forks. Bear ➔ and continue climbing.

5 Keep to the distinct rutted track and pass through a couple of gates – the track becomes more obvious towards the top. Eventually you reach the plateau and are treated to superb views ahead. Keep going ⬆ on the main trail as it dips

Passing the old kiln at Cote

On the big final descent back to West Burton

over the other side of the fell and transforms into a fantastic descent. Very long, containing lots of rocky sections and twisting bends, this is a real treat, as well as a test. At the bottom the track emerges at a tarmac lane by an old kiln at **Cote**. Turn → and follow this lane back into **West Burton**.

7 The Dentdale Dalliance

START/FINISH	Public car park in Dent SD 704 870
DISTANCE	19km (12 miles)
OFF ROAD	9.5km (6 miles)
ON ROAD	9.5km (6 miles)
ASCENT	710m (2330ft)
GRADE	▲
TIME	3hrs–3hrs 30mins
PARKING	Large car park in Dent
PUB	The Sun Inn, Dent
CAFÉ	Meadowside Café, Dent

50%
OFF ROAD

With its cobbled streets and old-world charm, Dent, located in the heart of picturesque Dentdale, is an idyllic place to start a ride. A good tour of the northern half of Dentdale can be had by linking bridleways on Frostrow Fells with Occupation Road – known as 'Ocky Road' to some. While the going can be quite soft during rainy periods, the tracks over Frostrow Fells provide interesting riding and great views of the southern Howgills and Sedbergh. Occupation Road, which was once a notorious quagmire (due, in part, to 4x4 use), has been much improved by the Yorkshire Dales National Park Authority and gives good high-level scenic riding along the southern flank of Dentdale. However, this ride saves its best for last with the superb blast back into Dent down Flintergill. Steep, twisting, loose, rocky and with drainage ruts, there is plenty to keep you occupied on this white-knuckle thriller.

OVERVIEW

After a short road spin out of Dent, height is soon gained by a quiet tarmac lane past farm buildings and then a grassy walled byway. This soon opens onto moorland where the going can be a bit of a slog during wetter periods, as the ground does become fairly boggy here – however, it is never too bad to enforce long periods out of the saddle. Once the summit is reached, fun riding is had by descending Holebeck Gill and contouring around Frostrow Fell. Before long you descend to Side Farm and pick up tarmac again. A quick spin to Millthrop and you pick up

The Dales Way, which climbs steeply out of the peaceful hamlet. Good tracks take you back around the fell and a fun descent on a loose-surfaced track returns you into Dentdale. Once over the other side of the River Dee a short ride down the dale takes you to Gawthrop. From here a quad-crunching climb that gains more than 120m in just over 1km takes you to the head of Barbondale. You then pick up the Occupation Road track and ride high above Dentdale before the splendid final flourish of Flintergill returns you back into the heart of Dent.

DIRECTIONS

1 Starting from the car park in **Dent** turn → onto the road and ride **W** out of the village in the direction of Sedbergh. Cross Birks Bridge and continue along this road for around 20m before turning → onto a tarmac lane with a dead end sign.

2 Climb the narrow lane to meet a fork. Bear ← and keep climbing steadily past farm houses and ignoring footpath signs. At a fork by the entrance to **Hining Hall Farm** bear ← onto the rougher surfaced track and ride to meet the farm at Lunds. Bear ← to go around the side of the house and pass through a series of gates – the first is marked with a *no vehicles* sign. Continue along the rubble-strewn walled byway to meet a sorry-looking gate. Pass through and ride along the grassy and, in parts, boggy byway that runs parallel to the wall on your **left**.

3 Eventually the track leads to a gate. Pass through and turn sharp ← following the bridleway signed to *Frostrow*. The track soon dips and then leaves the drystone wall it has been following at a corner. Follow the obvious trail over grassy moorland and descend alongside Holebeck Gill. Keep to the main path as it levels and contours around the fell – it **can be vague** in places here. After a short while you will meet with a wider stone track.

Climbing steadily out of Dentdale

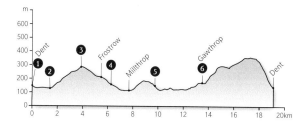

Follow this to descend to meet a gate with a laddered stile. Pass through and ride a short rocky section to emerge on tarmac by Side Farm.

4 Descend the tarmac lane and, as the gradient eases, turn ← at a fork following the sign to *Dent*. Soon you will ride into **Millthrop**. Pass through this quiet hamlet and turn ← to climb the stone-surfaced track signed to *Frostrow Fell*. This path, which forms part of The Dales Way, gives a short but steep test of your climbing legs. The gradient eases round the **LH** corner. Drop to ford a small stream and then bear ← following *The Dales Way* sign and climb steeply again for a short distance to meet a pair of gates. Choose the → option to stay on The Dales Way and follow this obvious bridleway as it passes through several gates and drops past Gap Wood to emerge by a farm at **Gap**.

5 Continue ↑ following a sign to *Brackensgill* and descend the walled track – a fun little blast. At a fork bear → to continue descending and emerge at a tarmac road. Go ↑ to cross the road, following a sign to *Brackensgill*. Cross the River Dee via the ford or nearby footbridge and ride to meet another tarmac lane at **Brackensgill**. Turn ← and ride along this undulating road alongside the river until you arrive in **Gawthrop**.

6 At a junction turn → to follow a sign to *Barbon and Kirkby Lonsdale*. Climb this steep hill into the top of Barbondale. From the summit descend a short distance to meet a bridleway turning on your **left** signed to *Dent and High Moss*. Take this wide and well-maintained track, which is known as Occupation Road, and ride high above Dentdale. When you reach a turning by fingerposts turn ← following the sign to *Dent via Flintergill*. Pass through the gate and begin the long, and increasingly steep, rocky and fast descent of Flintersgill. This twisting delight more than makes up for the earlier road climb. At the bottom go ↑ at a children's play area to emerge by the village car park and your starting point.

The start of the climb from Arncliffe Cote

8 Kilnsey and Mastiles Lane

Start/Finish	Kilnsey SD 974 678
Distance	19.25km (12 miles)
Off road	15.25km (9½ miles)
On road	4km (2½ miles)
Ascent	595m (1950ft)
Grade	▲
Time	2hrs 30mins–3hrs
Parking	On street in Kilnsey
Pub	The Old Hall Inn in Threshfield is nearest (none en route)
Café	Kilnsey Park Fishery (but bring sandwiches as well)

The ancient Mastiles Lane has seen activity for thousands of years. The Romans camped here while campaigning in the area, the lane was used by monks in the period before the dissolution of the monasteries and it was used by drovers to move cattle in the intervening periods. Mastiles Lane also makes for an excellent mountain biking track and this route uses the lane in the return leg of a classic loop starting from Kilnsey. By travelling from west to east along the lane bikers can enjoy the superb high-speed descent of Mastiles Lane into Wharfedale – one of the most enjoyable descents in the national park.

Overview

The short tarmac ride from Kilnsey to Arncliffe Cote is all the road you will see on this ride. The remainder of the route is entirely off-road on well-worn bridleways and byways. A long climb from Arncliffe Cote soon takes you away from civilisation and onto the moors high above Littondale. Once the high point is reached, a long fun descent, and a short flat section of trail takes you to the start of Mastiles Lane, near Malham Tarn. The wide and firm surfaced Mastiles Lane provides easy riding and the miles are soon clicked over before you reach the start of the descent back towards Kilnsey. The top section has a short loose rocky section but after this the descent is mostly free from technical difficulties.

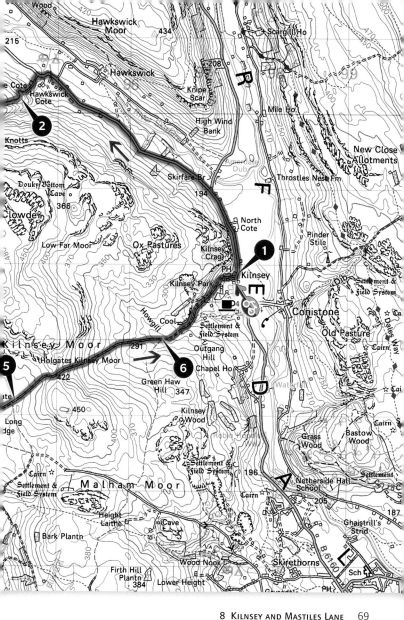

Directions

1 From **Kilnsey** head **N** along the `B6160`, passing **Kilnsey Crag**. Turn ← at the first junction – signed to *Arncliffe and Litton* – and continue riding to meet a bridleway turning on the **left** signed to *Street Gate*. Take this bridleway and ride along the tarmac surface to meet buildings at **Arncliffe Cote**.

2 Continue ↑ as the track surface deteriorates beyond the barn and follow the bridleway as it climbs to a gate. Pass through and continue climbing as the obvious grassy track zig-zags up a couple of hairpins and then rises steeply onto **High Cote Moor**.

3 Climb parallel to the deep gully on the **left**. Keep following the bridleway ↑, passing through several gates. The track is well signposted. Keep following the signs to *Street Gate* as the trail snakes upwards to the summit at High Lineseed Head.

Thermal gear helps on winter rides

A wintry Mastiles Lane

From here the path descends and passes through a couple more gates. Keep descending on the obvious path to ford a stream by a wall and pass through another gate.

4 The track flattens and after a short distance arrives at a signed junction by a gate at **Street Gate**. Do not pass through the gate and instead turn ←, following the sign for *Kilnsey* – you are now on Mastiles Lane. Ride along this broad walled track a short distance and then drop to meet a gate and ford a stream. Continue riding and if you look right you can see the top of **Gordale Scar**, which was made famous by a Turner painting. Continue ↑, passing through the site of a Roman camp (marked by a sign) until you meet a junction of bridleways at a gate. Ignore the right option and keep going ↑.

5 Climb briefly then drop at pace to meet another junction by a gate. Continue ↑, passing through the gate, climb a short distance and catch your breath before savouring Mastiles Lane's stunning finale. This long, fast and furious descent is initially rocky but then smoothes out to encourage high speeds to the gate at the bottom.

6 Pass through the gate and continue ↑ to follow the track as it drops again to meet a tarmac lane. Follow this lane to plunge steeply back into **Kilnsey**.

Tricky singletrack riding off Fremington Edge

9 Fremington Edge

START/FINISH	Fremington SE 046 986
DISTANCE	21km (13 miles)
OFF ROAD	15km (9¼ miles)
ON ROAD	6km (3¾ miles)
ASCENT	700m (2300ft)
GRADE	▲
TIME	3hrs–3hrs 30mins
PARKING	Dales Bike Centre, Fremington
PUB	The Red Lion, Langthwaite
CAFÉ	Dales Bike Centre, Fremington

This cracking little route that circumnavigates Reeth takes in the most prominent geological feature of this corner of the Dales – Fremington Edge. Although starting with a very tough climb up the face of the Edge, this route also packs in two fantastic descents and a scenic cruise alongside the River Swale; thus providing the key ingredients of views, atmosphere and adrenaline that make Dales riding so special.

OVERVIEW

The legs are brutally warmed up by the ferociously steep climb up the face of Fremington Edge from the hamlet of High Fremington. A short descent from the top to Hurst then leads to more gradual climbing as the route follows a track that meanders through old mining ruins. The descent from the hidden gate at the summit is awesome. Long, fast, varied and containing drop-offs and switchbacks, this plunge to Storthwaite is a real favourite. After passing through Langthwaite, and undertaking a short section of road, more off-road climbing then leads to a nice section of singletrack over moorland, before another fine descent drops you back into Swaledale. After crossing to the far side of the River Swale a pleasant bridleway along the banks of the river is followed to Grinton and a short spin back to the start.

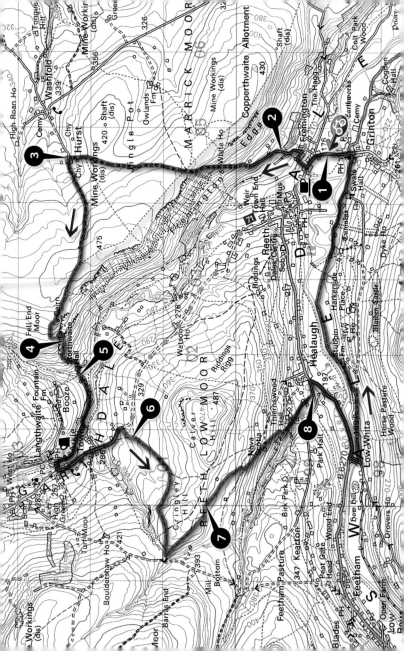

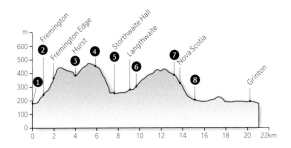

Danger – if the River Swale is in spate and covers a significant portion of the cobblestones on the bridleway to Grinton then retrace your steps and follow the tarmac lane instead. Riders have been known to get into difficulties here when the river is up.

DIRECTIONS

1 Turn ← out of the Dales Bike Centre and ride in the direction of Reeth. Take the second turning →, signed to *High Fremington*. Climb steeply to meet a T-junction among houses and turn ← to continue climbing. Keep to this tarmac lane as it rises steeply to the face of **Fremington Edge**.

2 Eventually the tarmac gives way and is replaced by a loose rocky bridleway – unfortunately the gradient remains relentless. Pass through a gate and keep climbing to meet a fork by a cairn. Bear ← and follow the track to meet a gate in a wall at the top of Fremington Edge. Pass through and enjoy the descent on the other side along a wide rocky path that winds its way to the hamlet of **Hurst**.

3 At the tarmac lane turn ← following the bridleway sign. The tarmac soon gives way to a wide gravel track. Keep to this main path as it passes through the spoil heaps of old mining works. The track gradually climbs until it reaches a seemingly dead-end at a wire fence. The track actually swings **left** and runs along the drystone wall. Follow this to meet a gate hidden behind a kink in the wall and pass through.

4 Descend along the trail ahead as it drops down into **Arkengarthdale**. This path soon becomes vague but keep following the cairns and yellow bridleway posts. The bridleway eventually swings **left**, transforming into sublime singletrack that hugs the side of the fell as it begins to descend – **watch out for rocky drop-offs**. Follow the track as it zig-zags in its continual descent and passes through a gate in a wall. Continue dropping down the side of a grassy field, which contains more switchbacks, before emerging at a gate by **Storthwaite Hall**.

5 Turn → onto the track at the bottom, ford a beck, and follow the bridleway adjacent to Arkle Beck to reach **Langthwaite**. At Langthwaite turn ← opposite the Red Lion and then ← again onto the road back to Reeth. Pass through the inappropriately named hamlet of **Arkle Town** (there are only three houses) and keep riding to cross a cattle grid. Ignore the bridleway sign immediately on your right and keep riding a short distance further to reach an inconspicuous stone-surfaced track on the **right**. Turn on to this.

6 The track forks immediately. Take the ← fork and ride along this double-track path as it climbs steadily over the moor. Near the end of the track it drops to meet a drystone wall around 20m before a gate. Turn sharp ← onto a singletrack bridleway that forks from the main track by the wall (**easy to miss**). Follow this excellent path as it meanders across the moor. This section can be wet and muddy during rainy periods but remains very rideable.

The spectacular drop into Arkengarthdale

The steep descent to Storthwaite Hall

7 Ride to meet a fork by a bridleway sign near the corner of a wall. Bear → and ride a short distance to meet another track. Pass straight over to continue descending and ride to emerge by a house at **Nova Scotia**. At the far side of the house turn →, passing between small rocks to continue descending, this time on grassy singletrack. Pass through the gate at the bottom, go across a small field and then through the gate on the far side. Follow the bridleway to emerge on a loose stone-surfaced driveway. Descend this and bear ← at the tarmac lane at the bottom.

8 Follow the lane to meet a T-junction and turn → onto the `B6270` just before the village of **Healaugh**. Turn first ← to cross the **River Swale** and turn ← again on the far side. Ride along this narrow tarmac lane until meeting a fingerpost on the start of a bridleway signed to *Grinton*. Turn ← onto this bridleway and follow this excellent track as it runs alongside the river, passing through several gates. After a cobbled section the trail leaves the side of the river, passing over a field, but remains obvious. Keep riding along the bridleway, passing through more gates, until you emerge at a tarmac lane in **Grinton**. Turn ← then ← again at the T-junction. Bear ← at the junction with the `B6270`, opposite The Bridge pub, and ride the short distance back to the Dales Bike Centre.

Descending the fearsome Bunton Hush

10 Gunnerside

START/FINISH	Gunnerside SD 950 981
DISTANCE	19km (12 miles)
OFF ROAD	15km (9½ miles)
ON ROAD	4km (2½ miles)
ASCENT	855m (2805ft)
GRADE	◆
TIME	3hrs–3hrs 30mins
PARKING	Spaces by Gunnerside Beck in village
PUB	King's Head in Gunnerside
CAFÉ	Ghyllfoot Tea Room in Gunnerside

80% OFF ROAD

This is a great route that contains two cracking descents – one fast and furious, the other highly technical that will test riders' skills to the limits. Making use of riverside byways, mining tracks and bridleways over open pasture, despite its short distance this route is packed with variety and atmosphere. Its high off-road percentage also means you should allow for a bit more time than you would for other rides of this length.

OVERVIEW

A short tarmac descent from Gunnerside soon takes you to the first off-road section – a long riverside track that can be very muddy during wet periods. This is followed by a long tarmac climb to Surrender Bridge and then onto old mining tracks that take you over the moorland high above Swaledale. From

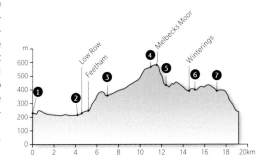

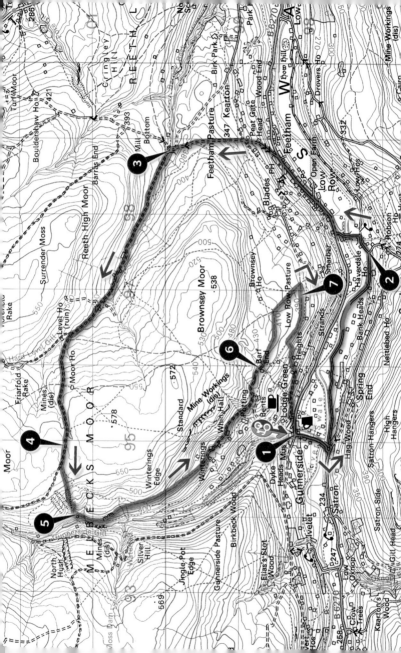

the top of the moor the highly technical descent of Bunton Hush drops you into Gunnerside Gill. From here a cracking bridleway along Winterings takes you to Barf End Bridge. Three more bridleways over fields then deliver you to the start of the descent back into Gunnerside – an absolutely storming blast along a twisting lane with sections of loose rocks to keep you alert.

Directions

1 Head **S** out of **Gunnerside** along the `B6270` following Gunnerside Beck. Cross the River Swale and turn first ← signed to *Crackpot*. Bear immediately ← on to a gated byway and follow this rocky and muddy track alongside the river for almost 2.5km and emerge on a tarmac lane.

2 Turn ← at the T-junction by a bed and breakfast and cross the River Swale again. Climb to another junction and turn → onto the `B6270` signed to *Reeth*. Pass through **Low Row** and ride to meet the Punch Bowl pub in **Feetham**, then turn ← – signed *Langthwaite* – and begin to climb the very steep lane ahead. The gradient eases soon after crossing a cattle grid and the road continues climbing steadily onto open moorland. Follow the road as it drops to cross a beck at Surrender Bridge and then turn ← onto the signed bridleway.

Riding alongside Old Gang Beck

Rocky mining spoils provide interesting riding near Gunnerside Gill

3 Climb steadily along this wide gravel-surfaced track alongside Old Gang Beck to pass old mine works. Bear ➜ at a fork following the sign to *Level House Bridge*. At the next fork turn ⬅ to cross the bridge and continue climbing on the main track – ignore all turnings.

4 The path dips slightly before rising again and reaching a plateau on **Melbecks Moor**. Ride to meet a small stone cairn as the track swings to the **right**. Bear ⬅ and head to the larger cairn a short distance away. Turn 90° ➜ at the cairn and look for the start of a small gully on your **left**. Keep just ⬅ of the gully and descend steadily alongside it. Just past a bridleway sign the hill steepens. Drop down this slope and then bear ➜ to drop into Bunton Hush gully itself (**do not venture into the more obvious left-hand gully straight ahead**). Drop down this very steep, rocky and highly technical singletrack descent to meet a T-junction with another bridleway at a fingerpost at **Gunnerside Gill**.

5 Turn ← and follow the obvious track to meet a fork by a cairn. Turn ← (the right-hand fork is a footpath) and ride along the bridleway as it contours along **Winterings Edge**. Keep to the main path as it passes the cottages at Winterings and continues to reach a fork by a gate at the top of a tarmac lane on your right. Ignore this turning and continue ↑ on the bridleway to reach **Barf End** gate.

6 Turn ← just before the gate and follow the faint bridleway (**can be vague – if in doubt follow the wall to your right**) and ride above the piles of rocks to meet a gate in the wall. Pass through and bear slightly ← heading to the track marked by a wooden post. Follow this boggy bridleway to meet a wide grassy track by a wall. Turn →.

7 Follow this track to meet a gate. Pass through and bear immediately ← to enjoy a long, fast, twisting and exhilarating blast down towards Gunnerside – a cracker. Keep to the main track and ignore all turnings. Eventually you will come out onto a steep tarmac lane. Turn ← and descend to an electric gate. Pass through and turn → on to the `B6270` in **Gunnerside** to return to the start.

Riding along the terraced track by Gunnerside Gill

Plunging into spectacular Littondale (Route 19)

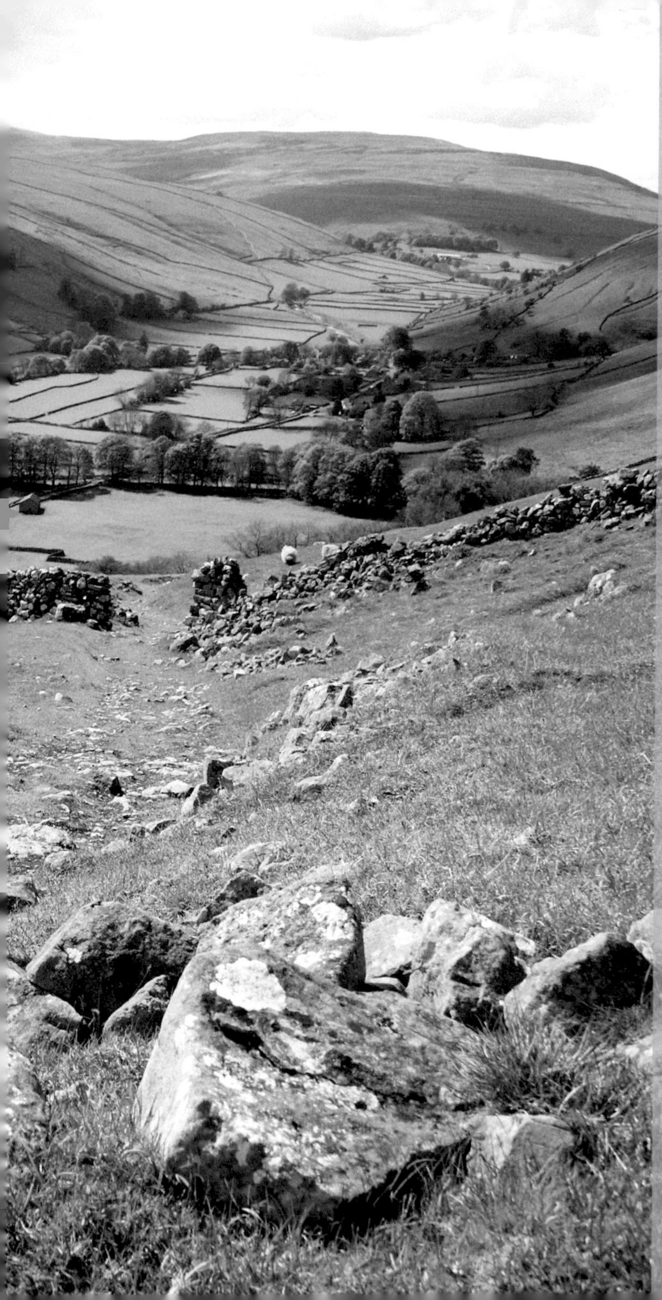

MEDIUM LOOPS

Descending the fun Moor Lane track

11 Hetton Hijinks

START/FINISH	Hetton SD 961 587
DISTANCE	25km (15½ miles)
OFF ROAD	20km (12½ miles)
ON ROAD	5km (3 miles)
ASCENT	600m (1970ft)
GRADE	■
TIME	3hrs–3hrs 30mins
PARKING	On street in Hetton
PUB	The Angel, Hetton
CAFÉ	Bring sandwiches

This route, which takes in the bridleways north of Hetton, is an excellent loop on well graded trails that provide interesting and varied riding that is not too technically demanding. Set in a peaceful and picturesque corner of the Dales, this is a ride that can be enjoyed all year round and is a good option for the less experienced – and more experienced riders will enjoy the cracking riding on offer too.

OVERVIEW

The route leaves the village of Hetton via a hidden bridleway that passes between houses and swiftly becomes a fun singletrack descent. After passing through Rylstone and the edge of Cracoe the route loops around the back of Swinden Quarry on enjoyable bridleways. A short road spin is followed by a long climb onto Threshfield Moor. Good, well-maintained tracks, weave an undulating route across the moor to meet a quiet tarmac lane. A short ride soon brings you to the farm at Bordley, where more bridleway pedalling takes you through the farm at Middle Laithe. It is a short but steep climb from here to Weets Top. Satisfied that most of the climbing is now behind you, enjoy a long descent through several fields to an old stone bridge over Hetton Common Beck. One last short climb later and it is a long straight blast all the way back down to Hetton.

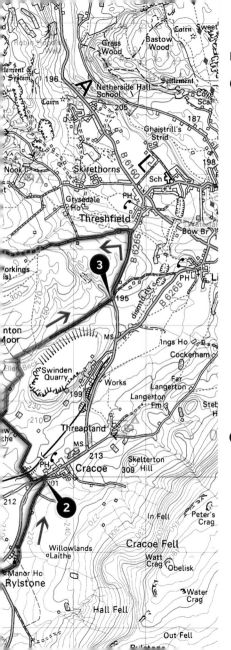

Directions

1 In the centre of **Hetton** find the grassy triangle in the centre of a junction of roads (there is a bench and large signpost inside it). From here take the bridleway running immediately SE between houses, signed to *Rylstone*. Enjoy a short singletrack descent beneath trees and then cross an old stone bridge and continue to emerge on tarmac. Turn → and ride to a T-junction. Turn ← onto the `B6265` and then immediately turn → onto a narrow lane signed to *Rylstone Church and Manor House Farm*. Ride to meet a junction with another bridleway and continue ↑ passing through a gate signed to *Cracoe*. Follow this walled lane as it drops to emerge back on the `B6265` at **Cracoe**.

2 Turn ← then first →. Then immediately turn → onto a bridleway signed to *Linton*. Pass under a railway and follow the track to two gates. Turn ← to follow the bridleway sign. Climb the steep singletrack trail and ride to another gate. Head to the **LH** corner of the wall directly ahead. Pass to the **RH** side of the stone barn ahead.

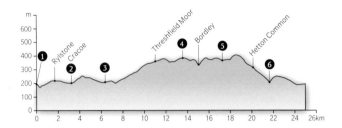

Then continue riding across the field ↑, heading to the **right** side of the copse on the far side. Drop to a steep-sided ford and climb the far bank onto **Linton Moor**. Then bear → and enjoy a twisting descent on a firm gravel-surfaced trail. Pass through a gate and continue your descent to pop out back on the `B6265`.

3 Turn ← and ride to the first turn ← signed *unsuitable for caravans*. Take this and climb the tarmac lane. Continue climbing as it becomes a stone-surfaced trail. Ride to a gate and bear → following the bridleway sign. Continue the long climb over **Threshfield Moor**, sticking to the bridleway signs, including forking ← at a fingerpost by a series of shooting butts. At a fork by a gate bear → following the sign to *Malham Moor Lane*. Keep following the obvious track as it crosses a series of wooden boards and past a stone barn to eventually emerge at a tarmac lane.

4 Turn ← and ride slightly uphill before descending to a junction. Turn ← following the sign to *Bordley*. Descend steeply to the farm at **Bordley** and ride to the gate in the far **RH** acorner of the farmyard. Pass through and climb steeply. Continue along the track as it levels out, passes through a gate, and descends around a hairpin bend. Bear → as the bridleway merges with a more distinct track and continue climbing to a gate. Pass through and ride ↑ to drop into the farm at Middle Laithe.

Fording a stream by Linton Moor

Climbing onto Threshfield Moor

5 Pass through the farm to reach the tarmac lane and ride along this until it begins to descend. Look for a hidden turning on the **left** signed *bridleway to Weets Top*. Take this and climb to a gate. Pass through and bear ← at the fingerpost junction, following the sign for *Hetton*. Descend to a gate, pass through and continue descending on fast singletrack over moorland. Pass through the next gate and follow the track as it cuts across the top of the next field and heads to a gate in the **RH** perimeter wall. Pass through, descend to another gate, go through again and drop to the bottom of the next field to emerge by a stone bridge.

6 Cross the bridge and climb the bridleway track on the far side to reach a junction by a gate overlooking **Winterburn Reservoir**. Pass through riding ↑ following the sign to *Hetton*. Stay on this wide walled track as it gives a long, fast and fun descent all the way back into **Hetton**.

Stopping to take in the magnificent views over Thieves Moss limestone pavement

12 Sulber, Wharfe and Feizor

START/FINISH	Horton in Ribblesdale SD 808 726
DISTANCE	26km (16¼ miles)
OFF ROAD	17.5km (11 miles)
ON ROAD	8.5km (5¼ miles)
ASCENT	550m (1805ft)
GRADE	■
TIME	3hrs–4hrs
PARKING	Pay and display in Horton in Ribblesdale
PUB	The Crown Inn, Horton in Ribblesdale or divert to the New Inn, Clapham
CAFÉ	Elaine's Tea Rooms, Feizor

The Yorkshire Dales is famous for its unique limestone pavements. This particular geological marvel is at its spectacular best in an area by Sulber called Thieves Moss. This fun ride around the fells between Ribblesdale and Clapham, with easy climbs and interesting descents, allows you to take in some of the best views of limestone pavement in the whole national park.

OVERVIEW
Starting from Horton in Ribblesdale, a gradual tarmac climb warms the legs and takes you to the first off-road section. From here you continue climbing at a mostly easy gradient across grassy fields (path finding can be tricky in the snow) past Sulber Nick and above Thieves Moss. Eventually the climbing stops and you are rewarded with a fast, rocky and fun descent down Long Lane. If you fancy an early pub stop you could divert to Clapham at the T-junction at the bottom of Long Lane – this is a good descent but you will need to climb back up the same way.

The next portion of the route consists predominantly of drystone walled lanes, which culminate in a cracking singletrack plunge into Wharfe. More singletrack and walled bridleway cruising soon brings you to Feizor and an opportunity for a cup of tea and a bite to eat at Elaine's Tea Rooms. After climbing out of peaceful Feizor a quick descent takes you to tarmac roads, which should be followed to Helwith Bridge and then back to Horton in Ribblesdale.

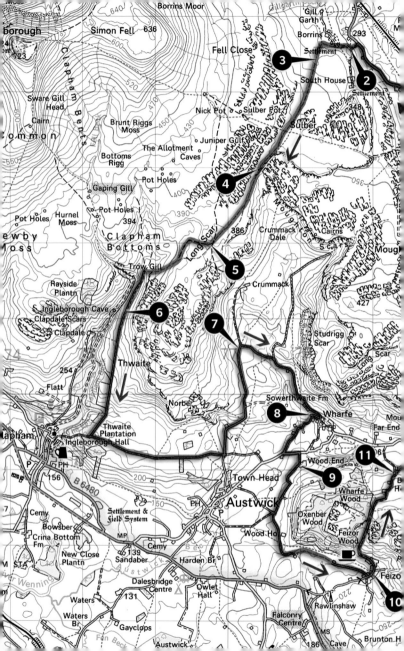

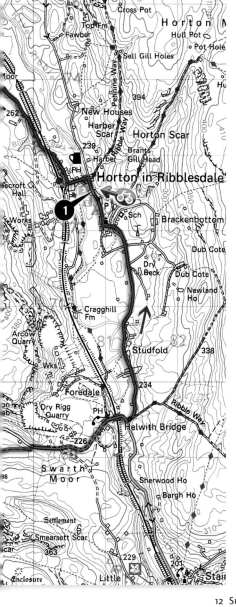

1 Leave **Horton in Ribblesdale** by riding **NW** along the B6479 towards Ribblehead. After climbing for around 2km turn ← at a sign for *South House Farm* onto a bridleway to Clapham.

2 The track climbs briefly to meet a fork – bear → and continue along the distinct track towards **Borrins Farm**. As the path swings **right** continue ↑ along a less distinct bridleway to meet a gate. Pass through this and, within metres, pass through another.

3 Continue ↑ along the grassy bridleway, ignoring all turnings. Go ↑ at a junction with a distinct footpath (with fingerpost) and ride on to a gate. Before passing through go to the fence on your left and take in the spectacular views over Thieves Moss limestone pavement.

4 Back to the ride, pass through the gate and carry on along the track. At a fork with a cairn bear → and continue ↑ to meet

Descending towards Wharfe

another fork. Bear ➜ again and follow as the trail swings off to the **right** into a cleft between hilltops.

5 Follow the obvious path to meet a gate. Pass through and drop across a field to another gate. Through this enjoy a fun descent down the aptly named Long Lane.

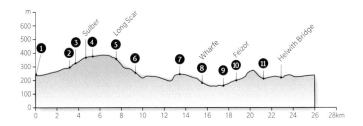

6 Follow Long Lane to a T-junction and turn ← towards Austwick. Ride along walled Thwaite Lane until it descends to meet a cross roads with a tarmac road. Turn ← and follow the road as it climbs **N** – the tarmac soon gives way to an unmade surface.

7 Turn → at a fork with a walled lane signed to *Wharfe*. Descend to pass over a picturesque stone bridge and continue ↑ on this excellent singletrack trail as it plummets to **Wharfe**.

8 At Wharfe turn →, passing houses, to meet another narrow bridleway. Follow this nice section of singletrack to meet a tarmac lane and turn ←. At **Wood End Farm** wall turn → onto a marked bridleway to *Feizor*.

9 Bear → at a cottage to stay on the walled bridleway. Continue along this track, ignoring gates and the first turning left, to meet a junction with three forks. Take the ← option. At the next building bear →, follow the bridleway to meet another fork and bear ← onto the *Pennine Bridleway* to **Feizor**.

10 At Feizor turn ← on the tarmac lane and continue through the village to meet a gate. Climb the main track and then descend to a gate. Continue ↑ descending the fast trail. Bear → at the cottage and continue descending. At the next cottage bear → and follow the path to another gate.

11 Pass through and follow the now grassy bridleway onto an open field. Continue ↑, crossing the field, to meet a gate on the far side. Pass through and climb a short distance to meet a tarmac lane. Turn → and ride to **Helwith Bridge**. At the T-junction with the B6479 turn ← and spin easily back to **Horton in Ribblesdale**.

The excellent singletrack on the return to Sedbergh

13 Cautley and Uldale

Start/Finish	Sedbergh SD 657 919
Distance	28.5km (17¾ miles)
Off road	17km (10½ miles)
On road	11.5km (7¼ miles)
Ascent	870m (2855ft)
Grade	■
Time	3hrs–4hrs
Parking	Main car park in Sedbergh
Pub	The Cross Keys Temperance Inn, Cautley ('dry' pub)
Café	The Howgills Bakery and Tea Room, Sedbergh (but bring sandwiches as well)

60% OFF ROAD

Taking in a picturesque hidden valley, one of the most spectacular waterfalls in the Yorkshire Dales, and mixing it with some great riding terrain – including a stretch of excellent singletrack – this route from Sedbergh makes for a highly enjoyable and scenic mountain bike ride. The going is generally good and although there are sections that can become boggy during wet times of the year, the mud is rarely too deep to prevent the progress of a determined rider with a good run-up.

Overview
Heading north-east from Sedbergh on the road towards Kirkby Stephen and the Eden Valley you approach the peaceful village of Cautley. Before entering the village you begin to climb high onto the fells that face the Howgills' eastern flank. The old byway here gives wonderful views over the impressive Cautley Spout waterfall, before a turn onto a bridleway takes you into the secluded Uldale valley – a little-known treasure for you to enjoy. After climbing out of Uldale a short tarmac stretch leads to a fast and furious descent over large rocks and across a ford – a particularly tricky section. A climb past Murthwaite leads to a short drop to Adamthwaite Farm. The bridleway running from here cuts high above the valley giving more spectacular views as well as interesting riding before dropping

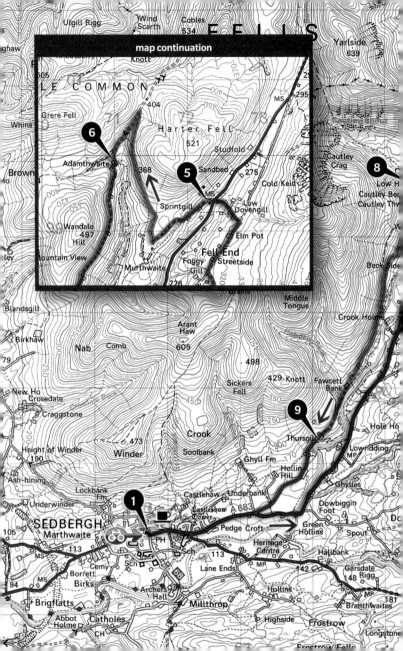

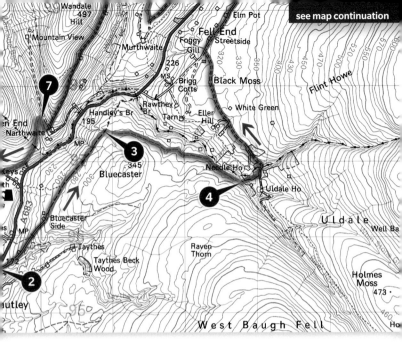

steeply over more rocks to Narthwaite Farm. The track then passes the Cross Keys Inn, a 'dry' pub run by Quakers that makes for a good rest stop. The bridleway forks from a footpath leading to Cautley Spout and gives a cracking long single-track return towards Sedbergh with only the last couple of miles being on tarmac.

Directions

1 Starting from the main car park in **Sedbergh** turn → out of the car park and then take the first → onto the `A683` towards *Kirkby Stephen*. Follow this road for almost 6km, passing Cautley Chapel and the parish church, to meet a fork on the **right** signed as a dead end. Take this.

2 Climb the narrow lane to meet buildings at **Bluecaster**, passing through a gate on the way. At Bluecaster the track forks, bear → (in effect ↑) and follow the stone and grass-surfaced byway that continues climbing ↑. Enjoy excellent views to your left of **Cautley Spout**. The byway gives mostly good riding despite one or two small boggy patches. Eventually the track forks at a bridleway sign – bear → to follow the bridleway arrow.

There are big views of the Howgills on the track from Bluecaster

3 Although quite boggy in many sections, this track gives generally fun riding as the boggy bits are never deep enough to force a dismount and, if anything, enhance the interest. Keep following the obvious path as it heads deeper into scenic **Uldale**. Eventually, as the track forks, bear ← and drop a short distance to meet a bridge by a small waterfall – a wonderful spot.

4 Cross the bridge and climb the track ↑. At the top turn ← onto a concrete double-track lane and follow to meet a gate. Pass through and follow the now tarmac lane to a T-junction and turn →. Follow this road to meet a ← turn signed *Byway to A683*. Descend this initially tarmac byway, which soon deteriorates and becomes littered with large rocks. Bear ← at a fork part way down and continue as the track merges with a stream. Keep going to ford another stream and emerge at the `A683`.

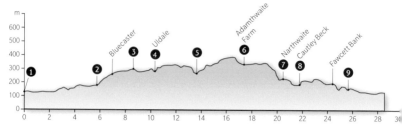

5 Pass ↑ over the road and climb the narrow lane opposite – signed *byway to Murthwaite*. Continue along the byway as its surface changes from tarmac to stone and steepens before levelling out again. Turn → at a fork with a bridleway sign and climb the long track to meet a tarmac lane. Turn ← and descend steeply to **Adamthwaite Farm**.

Rocks and water make for a tough balancing act

6 Bear ← and pass through the farmyard, continuing ↑ onto a good bridleway that cuts along a terrace high above the valley. Continue past the ruins of a stone dwelling and then descend a narrow rocky path. The track then becomes wider and muddier before dropping again to meet a junction of bridleways. Turn ← and descend very steeply over large rocks to reach **Narthwaite**. Enter the farmyard and turn → to exit through a gate.

7 Keep descending, passing through a couple more gates, to reach a ford. Cross and continue along the obvious track as it drops again to run along the **River Rawthey**. When you see Cautley Spout ahead, bear ← to cross a narrow wooden bridge.

8 Keep following the obvious narrow singletrack path as it hugs the fellside. After crossing a very small bridge bear → to continue along the path as it climbs the fell slightly. Keep to this main path through several more fields to eventually emerge by buildings at **Fawcett Bank**. The track now becomes wider and gives good riding before becoming a tarmac surface.

9 Descend this lane to meet the `B683` and turn →. Follow this road to retrace your way back into **Sedbergh**.

Wooden boards cross the boggy bits near Malham Moor

14 South of Mastiles Lane

START/FINISH	Airton SD 902 592
DISTANCE	29km (18 miles)
OFF ROAD	24km (15 miles)
ON ROAD	5km (3 miles)
ASCENT	790m (2590ft)
GRADE	■
TIME	3hrs–4hrs
PARKING	On street in Airton
PUB	The Buck in Malham is nearest (none en route)
CAFÉ	Bring sandwiches

85%
OFF ROAD

The south Dales is most well-known for its two famous landmarks – Malham Cove and Gordale Scar. These impressive geological features have been drawing visitors to the area for centuries, most famously perhaps in the case of the painter JMW Turner. The area surrounding these marvels is criss-crossed by a large network of paths, many of which are ideally suited for mountain biking adventures. This fine route links the ancient byway of Mastiles Lane with bridleways that explore this wonderful corner of the national park and throws three fun descents into the mix.

OVERVIEW

An easy spin north out of Airton takes you to Kirkby Malham and the beginning of the first climb of the day – a tarmac drag through the peaceful hamlet of Hanlith. From here you pick up an old byway that continues climbing, initially on a walled track and then over an open field. At the top you emerge on a recently maintained track and continue gaining altitude to reach the summit of Weets Top. A long descent ensues, passing through several fields, and ensures a wide grin at the bottom, where you cross a stream. A series of bridleways, which continue to climb steadily and undulate, take you along several fields, and across a couple of quiet lanes before another long descent drops you pleasurably to the foot of Mastiles Lane. A stiff climb up the face of Mastiles Lane will weed out those lacking in fitness. From here it is a short, interesting ride to reach Weets Top for a second time. A different descent is

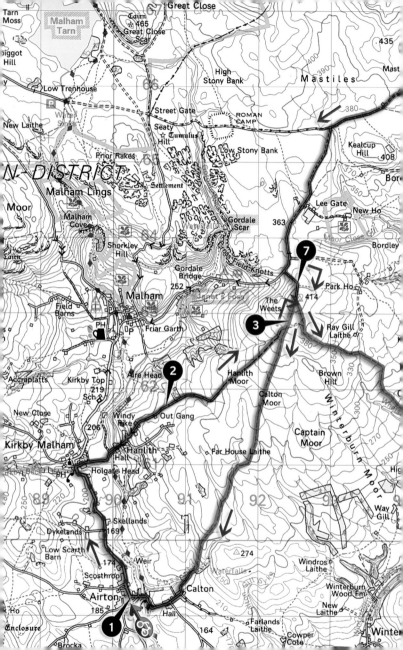

enjoyed to take you at pace into Calton, which is followed by a short tarmac ride back to Airton.

DIRECTIONS

1 From the centre of **Airton** ride **N** along the main tarmac road to **Kirkby Malham**. After a short descent turn → opposite a medieval church following the sign to *Hanlith*. The gradient soon steepens to give a stiff climb that zig-zags through the houses of Hanlith. At the top of the lane the tarmac gives way and the route ahead is on an unmade walled track called Windy Pike Lane.

2 Continue along the lane as it climbs at a slight gradient to reach a gate. Pass through and continue ↑ on the initially rocky and vague grassy track. Ignore a muddy path forking left and continue riding uphill across the centre of the field. The path passes over several drainage ruts and the occasional muddy patch before reaching a gate at the top corner of the field. Pass through and go ↑ a short distance to meet an obvious light-coloured bridleway. Turn ← and ride

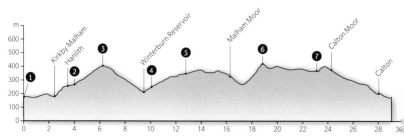

uphill to a junction with a fingerpost at **The Weets** top.

3 Turn sharp →, following the sign to Hetton and descend the fast well-made singletrack path as it drops to a gate. Pass through and continue descending to meet another gate. Go through again and ride across the top of the next field. Follow the bridleway as

Passing a stone barn near Malham Moor

it passes through another gate into the next field and then gives a fun and bumpy blast to the bottom of the hill. Keep following the sign for *Hetton* by crossing a small bridge and then climbing to meet a crossroads by a gate above **Winterburn Reservoir**.

4 Turn sharp ← following the sign to *Threshfield* and ride along this good stone-surfaced bridleway. After a short rocky section the track emerges at a tarmac lane. Turn ← then first → onto an obvious bridleway signed *Moor Lane Threshfield*. The track forks almost immediately. Take the ← fork (in effect ↑) and follow this track, which becomes grassier and soft for a short section. The track meets a gate by a fork. Turn ← following the sign to *Malham Moor Lane*.

5 This undulating track passes through several gates and over a few small wooden bridges before passing a stone barn and meeting another tarmac lane. Pass straight over and through the gate opposite to stay on the bridleway signed to *Kilnsey*. After a short climb enjoy a long and fast descent over **Malham Moor** to meet Mastiles Lane – **watch out for hidden rocks and ruts that threaten an unscheduled spill**. Turn ← onto Mastiles Lane and climb the imposing ascent ahead.

6 Continue ↑ along Mastiles Lane at the next two junctions with bridleways and then look for a sign on the **left** for *Lee Gate*. Take this turning and climb briefly before dropping to meet a tarmac lane by the farm at **Lee Gate**. Follow the lane until it starts descending, then turn immediately ← onto a stone-surfaced walled bridleway signed to *Weets Top*.

7 Climb to meet the signed fork at **The Weets** top again and this time bear → following the sign for *Calton*. Enjoy a long, steady and fast (if there is not a strong westerly wind) descent along this singletrack path. After passing through a gate the track becomes more vague but follow it as it undulates a short distance over pasture before continuing its fun descent into **Calton**. On reaching a tarmac T-junction as you leave the village turn → and drop back into **Airton**.

Descending off Weets Top towards Winterburn Reservoir

Entering steep-sided Barbondale

15 Barbondale and Lunesdale

15

START / FINISH	Kirkby Lonsdale SD 617 782
DISTANCE	25km (15½ miles)
OFF ROAD	13.5km (8¼ miles)
ON ROAD	11.5km (7¼ miles)
ASCENT	610m (2000ft)
GRADE	▲
TIME	3hrs–4hrs
PARKING	Free car park east of Devil's Bridge
PUB	The Barbon Inn, Barbon
CAFÉ	The Cariad, Kirkby Lonsdale

55% OFF ROAD

The Lune Valley, particularly the stretch between Kirkby Lonsdale and Sedbergh, is arguably one of the most beautiful landscapes in England. This route provides a good tour of the area, taking in the best bridleways on both flanks of the dale and allowing for widespread views over this charming countryside. This is an excellent ride on mostly easy tracks, though the technical descent into the more remote Barbondale makes this ride more worthy of a red grade than blue. The driveway of Barbon Manor is occasionally used as part of a local motor racing route, so before heading out go to www.westmorlandmotorclub.co.uk to check for and avoid any race dates.

OVERVIEW

The first half of the ride consists of quiet bridleways and a long road climb onto Casterton Fell before dropping into Bardondale – another spectacular dale, this one more rugged with steep-sided fells towering high above. A fast descent through the trees surrounding Barbon Manor takes you back into Lunesdale. A picturesque crossing of the river takes you to the other, less steep side of the valley and good bridleways, which include fun singletrack sections, provide an interesting and enjoyable return to Kirkby Lonsdale.

Directions

1 Starting from the free car park just east of Devil's Bridge, take the narrow tarmac path climbing from the rear of the car park. At the end of this path you emerge at the gated entrance to a caravan site – turn ← onto the adjacent bridleway. Follow this singletrack path to a junction of bridleways by a golf course. Turn → signed *High Casterton*.

2 At a T-junction in the hamlet of **High Casterton** turn → then immediately ←. Pass under the disused railway and climb to meet another T-junction. Turn → then first ← again onto a bridleway signed to *Fell Road*. Ride to meet a gate next to houses at **Bindloss Farm**. Pass through and bear →. Follow the bridleway as it then swings **left** along a grassy walled lane. Follow this to another gate, pass through and turn ← to ride along another walled track that takes you to a tarmac lane.

3 Turn → onto Fell Road and endure the long, and initially steep, climb onto **Casterton Fell**. After around 4km you eventually drop to meet a junction of paths at the isolated **Bullpot Farm**, a popular spot for cavers. Turn ← onto the bridleway signed to *Barbondale*. Enjoy this long descent that, with plenty of ruts and large sections of loose rocks, will give your skills a stern test.

On the wide track to Barbon Manor

4 At the road turn ➔ then after a short distance turn ← at the bridleway sign
to ford **Barbon Beck** (alternatively walk across the nearby footbridge).
After crossing the beck bear ← and savour the descent through the trees
below **Barbon Manor**. The bridleway emerges on the steep Manor driveway
(**occasionally used in motor racing hill climbs – ensure you avoid race
dates**). Bear ← to descend the drive – but do not cross the beck again. Turn
➔ on the last bend before the beck and ride across the field to a small tunnel
under a disused railway. Continue over the next field to arrive at a T-junction
with a tarmac lane in **Barbon**. Turn ➔.

5 Follow this narrow back lane to meet a turning on the **left**. Take this equally narrow lane and ride to the first bend. Turn → here onto an unsigned singletrack byway. Ride along this to emerge on the `A683` and turn →. Take the first ← turning signed to *Old Town*. Cross the **River Lune** and climb the road on the far side. At the next T-junction turn ← and ride past the impressive **Rigmaden Park**. Just past the hall turn → onto a signed bridleway. Ride across the field and up into the trees beyond. Pass a ruined cottage and over the field behind – following the depression of the eroded bridleway to meet a gate.

6 Keep following this bridleway to emerge onto a narrow lane. Go ↑ (in effect ←) to pass behind the nearby farm buildings onto another bridleway. This soon becomes very narrow and gives a cracking singletrack descent to another tarmac lane at **Mansergh**. Turn → then next ← at the old Rigmaden School building. Pass in front of St Peter's church and follow the obvious bridleway over the next two fields to a gate.

7 Go through and continue along a wide bridleway, which undulates for a short while, before dropping to meet another tarmac lane. Turn → and follow to meet a junction at **Kearstwick**. Turn ← and follow this lane back into **Kirkby Lonsdale**. Ride straight through the town centre and turn ← at the `A65` to return to Devil's Bridge.

Climbing away from Rigmaden Park

Passing through a limestone escarpment above Wharfedale

16 Grassington

START/FINISH	Grassington SE 003 636
DISTANCE	27km (16¾ miles)
OFF ROAD	20.5km (12¾ miles)
ON ROAD	6.5km (4 miles)
ASCENT	740m (2430ft)
GRADE	▲
TIME	3hrs–4hrs
PARKING	Large car park in Grassington
PUB	The Fountaine Inn, Linton
CAFÉ	Cobblestones Café (but bring sandwiches as well)

This excellent ride from the charming village of Grassington takes you through two completely different, and historic, worlds that lie on opposite sides of the River Wharfe. On Grassington Moor you will pick your way through the remains of 19th-century iron ore mining, which give the area an eerie character. Yet over on Malham Moor you will ride through charming, rolling sheep pasture that is perhaps some of the most idyllic countryside in the region. Consisting of long gradual climbs followed by big, fast descents, this route provides a memorable action-packed day in the saddle that you will want to ride again and again.

OVERVIEW

This ride of two halves starts with a long climb out of Grassington onto the moor that bears its name. When the road gives way to a mining track the climbing just keeps coming until you reach the very top of the old lead mines. A pleasant ride through moorland then brings you to a cracking plunge all the way back down into Wharfedale and the village of Conistone. The route crosses the River Wharfe and heads to Kilnsey before climbing out of the dale again. A long grassy climb over sheep pasture is followed by fun bridleways and then a good rocky descent towards Threshfield. Quiet roads and easy bridleways are then linked together for the return leg to Grassington.

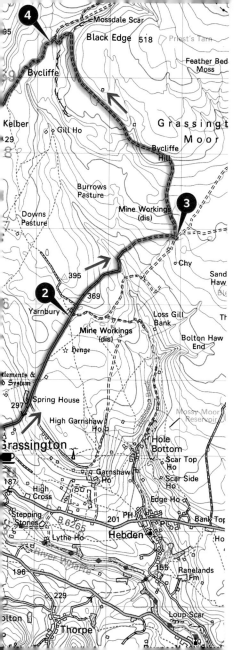

DIRECTIONS

1 Starting from the car park at the Yorkshire Dales National Park Authority building in **Grassington**, turn ← out of the car park. At the next junction (with Barclays Bank on the corner), turn → and climb through the busy town centre to meet a crossroads by the Town Hall. Continue ↑ to continue climbing Moor Lane – signed as a dead end.

2 Eventually this long climb takes you to a car park by buildings and an information sign explaining the area's lead mining history. Continue ↑ on the now stone-surfaced track, which climbs briefly before giving a good short descent. The trail then climbs again before snaking through remnants of the old mining activities. Follow this main path, ignoring all turnings, to meet an obvious junction of four distinct tracks. Take the ← fork (the track heading in the opposite direction to the chimney stack on your **right**).

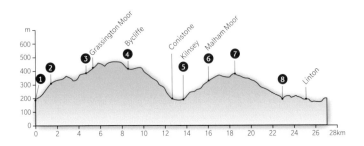

3 Follow this excellent track as it climbs steadily higher to take you above most of the mine workings. The path then dips briefly before climbing steeply up a short concrete section. The trail then levels out, passes through a gate, and after a short distance, drops to meet a bridleway T-junction.

4 Turn ← onto the bridleway and ride over the fairly level ground of **Bycliffe** to meet a gate. Shortly after the gate the long, fast and fun descent to Conistone ensues. Continue descending the main obvious trail passing through all gates. At the bottom turn ← onto the tarmac lane to ride into **Conistone**. In the village turn → signed to *Kilnsey*. Cross the **River Wharfe** and then turn → at the T-junction on the far side.

5 Ride into **Kilnsey** and turn ← onto a tarmac lane just after passing the Kilnsey Park Fishery. Climb the lane to meet a fork with an unmade track. Bear ← onto this path – signed *Route to Malham*. Ride to meet a junction at two gates and fork ← to leave Mastiles Lane and ride through a paddock. Pass through the gate and climb the grassy bridleway ahead to eventually meet a gate in a drystone wall.

On Grassington Moor – old enough to know better?

On the long bumpy trail towards Threshfield

6 Go through the gate and continue climbing to pass over the brow of the hill and descend to meet a gate at a tarmac lane. Proceed through this and go ↑ over the lane to go through another gate onto a bridleway signed *Boss Moor*. Ride on to go through several more gates. The trail becomes a sand-surfaced singletrack and passes over several small wooden bridges, giving fun riding, to meet another gate.

7 Ride along this walled bridleway to its end. Continue ↑, through a gate, ford a beck following the sign to *Moor Lane Threshfield* and *Boss Moor Lane*. After a short distance the bridleway forks at a gate. Bear ← following the sign to *Moor Lane Threshfield*. Enjoy a long, rocky descent, passing through a couple of gates, to emerge at a tarmac lane. Bear → (in effect ↑) and descend to meet a main road.

8 Turn → and climb briefly before descending. Look for a bridleway turn sharp ← signed *Linton* (**easy to miss**). Ascend this singletrack path to meet a gate. Through this the path widens and gives fast riding to meet another lane. Turn ← and ride through **Linton**, staying on this lane to meet a T-junction. Continue ↑ and follow the lane as it descends, bears **left**, and meets another T-junction. Turn → to pass back over the River Wharfe and climb up into **Grassington**. Keep riding on this road to reach the starting point.

Riding up the fine track onto Booze Moor

17 Arkengarthdale

START/FINISH	Langthwaite NZ 005 022
DISTANCE	27km (16¾ miles)
OFF ROAD	19km (11¾ miles)
ON ROAD	8km (5 miles)
ASCENT	995m (3265ft)
GRADE	▲
TIME	4hrs–5hrs
PARKING	Pay and display in Langthwaite
PUB	The Red Lion in Langthwaite
CAFÉ	Bring sandwiches

A ride of two halves, this route gives a thrilling tour of both flanks of Arkengarthdale – one of the most northerly of the national park's dales. Containing three excellent descents – including the cracking zig-zags down to Storthwaite Hall – this route first explores the westerly fells of the dale before moving eastwards, initially on tarmac, and then on fine gravel tracks over heather covered moorland, and later the eerie landscape of abandoned 19th-century lead mines. Although not particularly long in distance, and entirely rideable, this route can take longer than you may expect due to the significant amount of climbing involved.

OVERVIEW

Not long after leaving Langthwaite the climbing begins in earnest with a steep pull up a grassy and energy-sapping bridleway. The next section of bridleway continues the climbing, albeit at a more comfortable gradient, on to Whaw Edge. After passing through piles of old mining spoil, the first descent of the day – a fast, twisty screamer – drops you back down into the dale below. A tarmac spin takes you along peaceful and scenic lanes through, and then above, Whaw and then to Stang Bridge. A lengthy tarmac climb brings you to a wide track that meanders beneath a fine wall of crags with expansive views of Arkengarthdale and over to Swaledale.

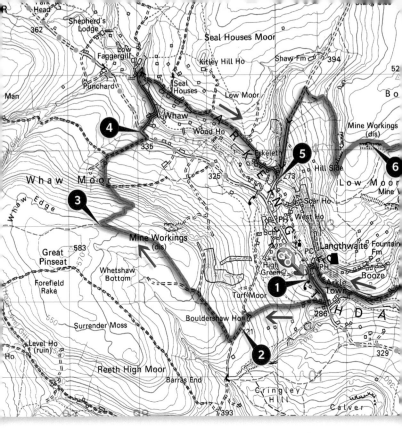

A long tour across moorland culminates in a fast drop to Schoolmaster Pasture before you loop back to Hurst, pass through the old lead mines and on to the top of Fremington Edge. A superb rocky and technical descent from here returns you to the valley floor and a sedate spin alongside the river back to Langthwaite.

DIRECTIONS

1 From **Langthwaite** head **S** along the tarmac road towards Reeth. Not long after leaving the village, opposite a grey cottage, turn **→** onto a stone-surfaced bridleway – signed to *Bouldershaw House*. Continue climbing **↑** past a B&B as the track becomes grassy. When passing **Bouldershaw House** farm the path rises sharply to meet a tarmac lane. Turn **←**.

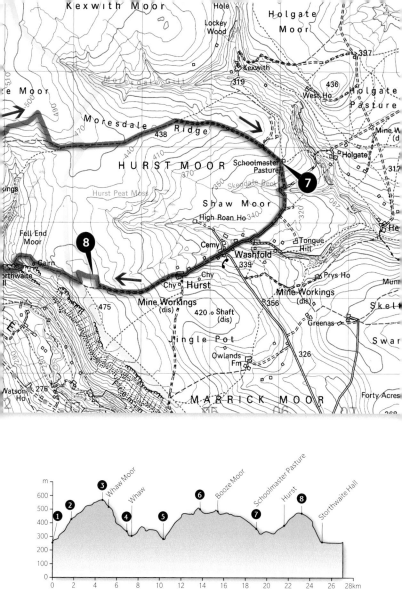

Climbing steeply out of Arkengarthdale

2 Climb a short distance to the brow of the hill and turn → onto a bridleway. Follow the gravel track and climb to a fork. Bear ← and continue climbing to meet another fork – bear →. Continue riding to reach mounds of mining spoil and follow the track as it bears to the **right** of the mounds before running in front of them along the top of the ridge.

3 At a series of three small stone cairns on the **RH** side of the track turn sharp → (almost back on yourself) and begin the long descent to the valley floor. Initially very loose and rocky, this soon becomes an excellent twisting blast. As the path levels out and meets a fork turn → and continue descending to meet a quiet tarmac lane.

4 Turn ← and then first →, descend to cross the stone bridge at **Whaw** and bear ← past Chapel Farm B&B. Follow the tarmac lane along the river and then continue along it as it climbs steeply and loops back across the fellside, passing **Seal Houses**. Continue ↑ and descend quickly (and carefully) to meet a T-junction by a beck at Stang Bridge.

5 Turn ← and begin the long climb of Stang Lane. On a brow of the ascent turn → onto a wide gravel bridleway opposite a small lay-by. Follow this trail as it rises beneath the crags. At a fork at a hairpin bend bear ← to stay on the main path (ignore straight ahead) and continue climbing for a short distance.

6 At the top stay on the main path as it descends a series of S-bends. At the bottom bear ← to stay on the more distinct track. Climb this gravel surfaced trail onto **Booze Moor** to meet a crossroads with another wide track. Turn → and descend this path to meet another crossroads. Turn sharp ← (do not continue descending) and follow this track to pass an upright stone. Stay on this main path as it then gives a long, gradual descent over Hurst Moor to the cottage at **Schoolmaster Pasture**.

7 Descend to meet a tarmac lane and follow this to a T-junction. Turn → and follow this to the road end at **Hurst**. Continue ↑, passing through a gate, and stay on the obvious main path as it climbs steadily through the scarred landscape of the former lead mine works.

8 The track eventually passes out of the former mining area, and at the hill top it seems to come to a stop by a wire fence. Bear ← and follow the stone wall to meet a hidden gate at 45° to the wall. Pass through the gate and continue ↑ on the bridleway as it begins to descend. Keep to the main track, which soon swings sharply to the **left** and gives a fantastic technical blast as it zig-zags down the side of Fremington Edge. Pass through a gate and continue the fun down a steep grassy field, through more zig-zags to meet another gate at the bottom by **Storthwaite Hall**. Go through, turn → and continue along the good path as it follows the river back to **Langthwaite**.

Massive heather moorland views over Booze Moor

The cracking blast back to Horton in Ribblesdale

18 Tour of Pen-y-ghent

START/FINISH	Horton in Ribblesdale SD 808 726
DISTANCE	28km (17½ miles)
OFF ROAD	17.5km (11 miles)
ON ROAD	10.5km (6½ miles)
ASCENT	690m (2265ft)
GRADE	▲
TIME	3hrs 30mins–4hrs
PARKING	Pay and display in Horton in Ribblesdale
PUB	The Crown Inn, Horton in Ribblesdale
CAFÉ	Pen-y-ghent Café, Horton in Ribblesdale

65%
OFF ROAD

This is a classic route around one of the famous three peaks, Pen-y-ghent. Although the route can be ridden in both directions, an anticlockwise tour provides the most rewarding experience with two stunning descents – first into Littondale and then the final plunge back into Horton in Ribblesdale. A very short stint of pushing will be required on the climb from Foxup, however this is not particularly arduous and the rest of this excellent ride more than compensates for your efforts.

OVERVIEW

An easy tarmac spin out of Horton in Ribblesdale leads to the first off-road section – a long straight climb towards the looming face of Pen-y-ghent itself. From the top, and following a short tarmac linking section, a long fun undulating track over Dawson Close leads to a fast and rocky descent into Littondale. Good stuff. A flattish road section then takes you to the hamlet of Foxup via Halton Gill. The next bit, however, is anything but flat. A very steep climb up onto Pen-y-ghent's eastern flank will test the legs and force the occasional dismount. When the track eventually levels out the riding is interesting over undulating ground. This route's finale is superb, with a long fast and furious blast all the way back into the heart of Horton in Ribblesdale on a wide firm surface – a guaranteed grin producer.

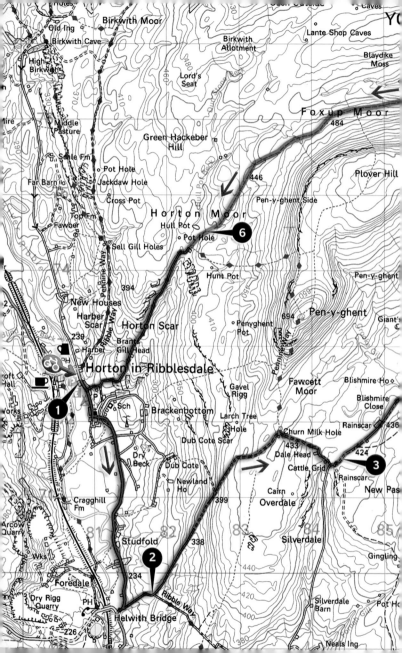

Directions

1 Ride **S** out of **Horton in Ribblesdale** on the `B6479` towards Settle. After around 3km, as the road begins to chicane to the **right** at a junction by **Helwith Bridge**, turn sharp ← onto a rocky byway signed to *Dale Head*.

It's a good drop into Littondale

2 At a fork bear ← continuing to follow signs for *Dale Head* and climb the walled Long Lane in the direction of **Pen-y-ghent**. Keep to the byway and follow it as it eventually relents and starts descending. At a fork bear → and drop to gates by a stone building. Continue past, and ride to emerge at a tarmac lane then turn ← on the *Pennine Way*.

3 Follow the road as it rises and then begins descending. Look for an off-road turning on the **right** signed *New Bridge*. Take this and follow the stone-surfaced double track byway as it undulates over **Dawson Close**. Shortly after fording a beck and passing an old limestone kiln, the track begins to descend. Despite a few gates this is an excellent plunge into Littondale – fast, wide and rocky. At the bottom, pass over an old stone bridge and ride to meet a tarmac lane and turn ←.

4 Ride the short distance to **Halton Gill** and then turn → (in effect ↑) following a sign for *Foxup*. On reaching the buildings at **Foxup** bear ← onto a signed bridleway to *Horton in Ribblesdale*. This is the hard bit. Climb steeply to a gate,

pass through and continue rising steeply over the next field – head for the gate high on the **right** side of the field. Pass through and continue climbing ahead to reach another gate. Go through and bear ← to ascend alongside the wall. After a particularly steep section the path reaches a small plateau. Follow the grassy track as it turns **right** at a right-angle away from the wall.

5 The track gives fine riding on a high terrace until you reach the second gate. The trail forks here. Ignore the easy option ahead as this is now a footpath. Instead the bridleway, which you follow, bears **left** steeply uphill in the direction of the sign pointing to *Horton in Ribblesdale*. This section forces a dismount and a short push (less than five minutes). The gradient soon eases and gives interesting riding to a gate. Pass through and continue ↑. Follow the obvious path over undulating terrain ignoring all turnings until the now grassy path descends to reach a T-junction with another bridleway. Turn → and descend to meet a gate.

6 Pass through and the route bears **left**. (Divert → to ride the short distance to visit the cavity of **Hull Pot** – take care as it's a big drop). Continue over flattish terrain to meet another gate by a junction with the Pennine Way. Pass through the gate and enjoy a long, fun and very fast descent back to **Horton in Ribblesdale** – however, **take extra care on this section as it is popular with walkers**. At a fork bear → to pass through a gate and descend to emerge on tarmac. Turn → to return to the car park.

Overlooking the impressive Hull Pot

Swooping into Littondale

19 Kettlewell and Old Cote Moor

19

START/FINISH	Kettlewell SD 967 722
DISTANCE	23km (14¼ miles)
OFF ROAD	16.5km (10¼ miles)
ON ROAD	6.5km (4 miles)
ASCENT	1040m (3410ft)
GRADE	◆
TIME	4hrs–5hrs
PARKING	Pay and display in Kettlewell
PUB	Queen's Arms, Litton
CAFÉ	West Winds Yorkshire Tea Room, Buckden

This ride may be short in length but its seemingly diminutive size packs a lot of action. Three big climbs are swiftly followed in turn by three stupendous descents that will have you grinning from ear to ear. Upper Wharfedale and Littondale are two of the most picturesque dales in the national park and this route links them by traversing the substantial bulk of Old Cote Moor. The climbs are steep and will force sustained pushes – however the fun of the descents more than makes up for any walking. Pick a good weather day to tackle this ride as low cloud may make navigation tricky on the climb of Old Cote Moor.

OVERVIEW

The ride starts as it means to go on with a very steep climb on a loose rocky bridle-way out of Kettlewell. From the top a brief section of level riding soon gives way to an exciting blast down a twisting walled track, with chicanes and hairpin bends, into Starbotton. A short road ride into Buckden then gives way to the biggest climb of the day onto Old Cote Moor. A steep start on a stony track leads to more gradual climbing on moorland, however the grassy surface makes the riding slow and arduous. The last section of the climb is too steep to ride and forces a push to reach the summit. However, the huge descent down the other side into Littondale soon makes amends. Rocky and technical at first, the descent then transforms into a bumpy and rutted track over grassy moorland. The trail becomes steeper again near the bottom, giving a fitting climax as it drops into Litton. A short ride

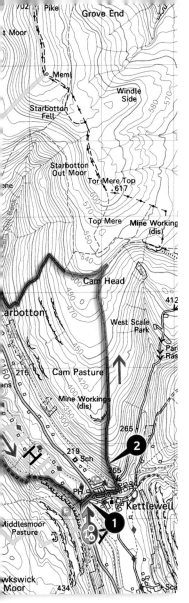

down the valley leads to another steep climb with technical sections near the top. Then another giant descent over grassy terrain and finally a very rocky track bumps and rattles you back into Kettlewell.

DIRECTIONS

1 From the pay and display car park by the River Wharfe in **Kettlewell** turn ← and ride into the village. Cross a small bridge and turn first →. Ride to a junction by Kettlewell Village Store and go ↑. Take the next turning ← signed to *Leyburn* and begin climbing. Then, at the next bend, continue ↑ onto the steep rocky bridleway ahead signed to *Starbotton and Coverdale*.

2 Climb steeply up the rocky track to meet a gate. Pass through and continue ↑ as the track levels. Continue along the wide path until meeting a fork with a fingerpost at **Cam Head**. Turn ← following the sign to *Starbotton*. After a short level section the trail soon begins heading downhill. Enjoy this terrific blast down the rocky and snaking bridleway, which plunges you into the heart of **Starbotton**. On reaching tarmac go ↑ and then turn → at the T-junction at the bottom.

3 Ride into **Buckden**. After passing The Buck pub turn ← at a fork following the sign to *Hubberholme*. After a short distance look for a bridleway sign on the **left** pointing the way to *Litton*. Begin climbing the initially

A tight hairpin on the cracking drop to Starbotton

steep stony track and continue following the bridleway as it becomes a worn singletrack trail over grassy moorland. Keep an eye out for the blue tipped wooden marker posts and keep to the faint trail that links them. The trail is rideable on the gentler lower slopes, however the gradient ramps up on the higher slopes and forces a substantial push. The final section has been paved and it is a short effort from the start of these stone slabs to the summit.

4 Continue ↑ and follow the rocky track as it passes through a gap in a wall. More paving slabs take you across the summit plateau and to a gate. Pass through and begin to pick your way down the immense descent into Littondale. **The top section is very steep, rocky and technical**. The next long section of this giant descent runs straight over bumpy grass. Eventually the

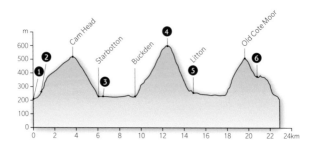

trail swings **right** to begin the final third of this cracking blast, a fast, twisting plunge down to meet a ford by a shady glade. Cross the ford and follow the bridleway sign ↑ to a gate. Follow the path and descend to emerge by the Queen's Arms pub in **Litton**.

5 Turn ← onto the valley road and ride for around 3km to the farm cottage of Old Cotes – dated 1630. Turn ← following the bridleway sign to *Starbotton*. The track climbs very steeply as it winds to a gate. Pass through and keep following the obvious track as it climbs to another gate below a hunting lodge. Through here the track forks, bear → following the bridleway sign. Keep climbing along the now technical trail to its summit by a gated wall. Pass through the gate and begin another huge descent down the other side. The descent is mostly over a bumpy grassy surface but **take care as it is also littered with unexpected drop-offs and hidden ruts**. After passing through the gaps of a couple of walls the bridleway eventually meets a junction at a gate.

6 Turn → and follow the bridleway to a gate in a wall to your **right**. Pass through, following the sign for *Kettlewell*. Continue along the bridleway as it runs around the upper side of an old farm building. On the other side of the farm the track soon starts its descent, a very tricky winding track with huge rock gardens that rattles you back into **Kettlewell**. Turn ← to cross the River Wharfe and return to the car park.

On the superb return to Kettlewell

Climbing onto Gorbeck with Pen-y-ghent looming on the horizon (Route 21)

LONG LOOPS

The fine Birkett Common byway

20 Kirkby Stephen and Crosby Garrett

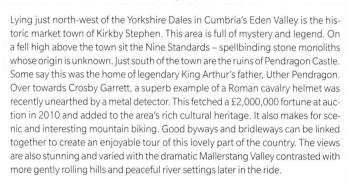

55%
OFF ROAD

START/FINISH	Kirkby Stephen NY 774 085
DISTANCE	33km (20½ miles)
OFF ROAD	18.5km (11½ miles)
ON ROAD	14.5km (9 miles)
ASCENT	670m (2200ft)
GRADE	■
TIME	3hrs 30mins–4hrs 30mins
PARKING	On street in Kirkby Stephen
PUB	The Croglin Castle Hotel, Kirkby Stephen
CAFÉ	The Midland Room, Kirkby Stephen station

Lying just north-west of the Yorkshire Dales in Cumbria's Eden Valley is the historic market town of Kirkby Stephen. This area is full of mystery and legend. On a fell high above the town sit the Nine Standards – spellbinding stone monoliths whose origin is unknown. Just south of the town are the ruins of Pendragon Castle. Some say this was the home of legendary King Arthur's father, Uther Pendragon. Over towards Crosby Garrett, a superb example of a Roman cavalry helmet was recently unearthed by a metal detector. This fetched a £2,000,000 fortune at auction in 2010 and added to the area's rich cultural heritage. It also makes for scenic and interesting mountain biking. Good byways and bridleways can be linked together to create an enjoyable tour of this lovely part of the country. The views are also stunning and varied with the dramatic Mallerstang Valley contrasted with more gently rolling hills and peaceful river settings later in the ride.

OVERVIEW

Quiet bridleways follow the River Eden south out of Kirkby Stephen, past medieval fortified homes, castle ruins and over pasture fields before a good byway takes you deeper into the Mallerstang Valley and almost to Pendragon Castle itself (a short diversion to visit the ruins is worthwhile). Height is gained by climbing steadily along a tarmac lane before open farmland is crossed by following another bridleway. More quiet lanes then take you across to Smardale Fell, which gives enjoyable riding and a fine descent to Scandal Beck. More nice bridleways are

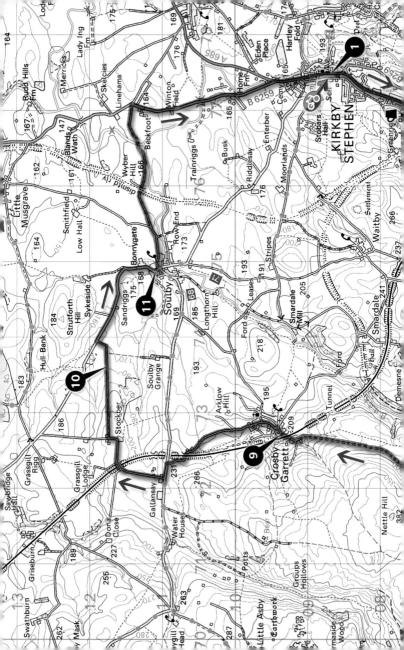

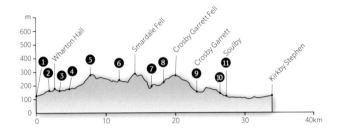

linked together to take you to Crosby Garrett Fell so you can enjoy the long and fast blast down into the village of the same name. A steady tarmac climb out of the village soon brings you to the start of the narrow bridleway descent of Mask Road. This is a fun descent through overhanging trees that has been improved by recent drainage works. The byway from Soulby will take you over the River Eden, where it joins Scandal Beck (a lovely spot) and a short road ride returns you into the heart of Kirkby Stephen and a deserved café stop.

DIRECTIONS

1 Head **SW** out of **Kirkby Stephen** on the `A685`. After passing the Station Garage (and attached bike shop) on the right you pass over a railway bridge. Just the other side of the bridge take the immediate turn ← onto the tarmac lane that climbs ahead.

2 Stay on this path as it turns into a concrete surface after a cattle grid and heads into farmland. After a short distance you will meet a signed junction with bridleways. Turn → signed *Bullsgill or Mire Close Bridge*. Ride along the grassy track, pass through two gates, and turn ← at a bridleway junction to drop into **Wharton Hall**. Bear sharp → and follow the concrete track to a fork just before Mire Close Bridge.

3 Bear → (in effect ↑) and pass over a cattle grid. Then turn immediately ←, go through a gate and ride over the grassy field, keeping to the **LH** perimeter until you reach a gap on the far side. Pass through and continue ↑ over the next field to a gate. Go across the next field and then follow the worn track over another, larger field to meet the ruins of **Lammerside Castle** and ride to the next gate.

On the lane rising steeply out of Mallerstang

4 Bear ← here and follow the distinct wide byway as it contours around **Birkett Common** above the River Eden to eventually meet a tarmac lane (if you divert ↑ here you can visit nearby **Pendragon Castle**). Turn → to climb the road. After the road dips briefly it begins climbing again. Ignore two signed bridleways on the right and climb to a cattle grid by a wall. Turn → here onto an unsigned bridleway and follow it along the nearside of the wall.

5 Continue alongside the wall, ignoring the more distinct track forking to the right. As the field begins to narrow, look for a faint trail leading to the small barn behind the wall on the **right** side of the narrowing field. From the barn the track becomes more distinct. Follow it beside the wall to emerge onto a quiet tarmac lane at **Moor End**. Continue along this lane to meet a T-junction and turn → onto the **A683**. After a short distance you meet another T-junction with the busier **A685**. Turn ← then turn first → back onto a quiet tarmac lane.

6 Ride along this straight lane until you reach a **RH** bend with a bridleway junction. Turn ← onto the bridleway signed *Coast to Coast Brownber*. Follow the rutted grassy track as it climbs onto open fields across **Smardale Fell**. The track soon drops to meet a junction of bridleways by a fingerpost. Bear → (in

Long and straight Stockber Lane

effect ↑) signed to *Smardale Bridge*. Descend this fun track, which becomes rockier towards the bottom, and cross the narrow stone bridge.

7 Continue ↑ and climb the bridleway as it runs along an eroded trough to meet **Friar's Bottom Farm**. At the building turn → onto a narrow walled bridleway signed *Ravenstonedale Moor*. Following a gate the track becomes wider. Follow this short distance to meet a junction of bridleways by farm buildings. Turn → signed *Bents* and ride up the farm track to reach **Bents Farm**.

8 Enter the farmyard and turn ← before the last barn to pass through two gates. Follow the track past a camping barn to a gate below large boulders. Climb the bridleway to meet a signpost. Go ↑ on a fairly vague path. After a short distance the path meets with a more distinct bridleway. Bear → onto this grassy track and follow it to meet a gate. Pass through and enjoy a long descent on an ever improving firm-surfaced wide bridleway as it plunges you into **Crosby Garrett**.

9 Continue through the sleepy village on a tarmac lane, keeping to the **left** of the small beck. Follow the lane as it climbs steeply out of Crosby Garrett, passing under a bridge, to meet a T-junction. Turn ← then take the first turning → onto a narrow lane signed *Stockber*. Pass over the railway and shortly after a 90° **LH** bend look for a bridleway on the **right**. Take this, signed to *Mask Rd*.

10 This track, Stockber Lane, is excellent, giving a speedy descent that soon turns into fun singletrack weaving through encroaching undergrowth. When you emerge at the tarmac road turn → and ride into **Soulby**.

11 In the village take the second turning ← before you reach the bridge over the river. Follow this lane, ignoring a bridleway turning on the right, to meet a fork on a bend with an unmade wide track signed *Byroad Winton*. Descend this track until just before you reach the river. The path goes **left** and runs along the riverbank to meet a footbridge. Cross to the other side and continue riding to meet a tarmac road. Turn → and follow this road to meet a T-junction with another road. Turn → here and ride back into **Kirkby Stephen**.

Climbing on the Pennine Bridleway out of Settle

21 Settle and Malham Tarn

Start/Finish	Settle SD 819 637
Distance	27km (16¾ miles)
Off road	22km (13¾ miles)
On road	5km (3 miles)
Ascent	700m (2300ft)
Grade	▲
Time	4hrs–5hrs
Parking	Pay and display in Settle
Pub	The Lion, Settle
Café	Settle Down Café, Settle (but bring sandwiches as well)

80%
OFF ROAD

This long route takes advantage of track improvements brought about by the Pennine Bridleway scheme. The section of trail over Gorbeck, once a boggy mire, is now a fast-flowing firm byway that provides good cruising. This route links that trail with a loop of the picturesque Malham Tarn and a superb return down the bumpy Stockdale Lane descent to give a grand tour of one of the Yorkshire Dales' most popular areas.

Overview

A stiff climb out of Settle on a good bridleway soon lifts you above Ribblesdale onto the plateau of Gorbeck. This excellent undulating path takes you across the moor to meet a tarmac lane above Malham Cove. A circumnavigation of Malham Tarn is then followed by more off-road climbing before an excellent descent of Stockdale Lane. Two more quiet bridleways are then picked up on the return leg to Settle.

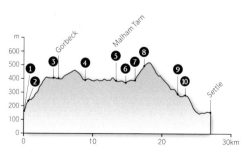

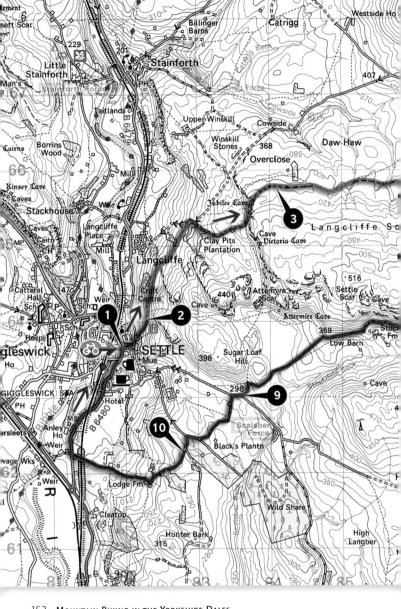

DIRECTIONS

1 Starting from the centre of **Settle** climb the steep road to the **left** of the Three Peaks bike shop in Market Place. Continue climbing Constitution Hill (signed) to meet a fork by a wall and trees. Bear → onto a stone and gravel surfaced bridleway and continue climbing steeply up the walled track to meet a gate.

2 Continue through the gate and along the bridleway as it crosses several fields to eventually meet the steep road that climbs from Langcliffe. Turn sharp → onto a gravel surfaced bridleway and climb as it winds up **Gorbeck**.

Riding above Ribblesdale

3 Keep following this good track as it meanders over the moor, passing through several gates, to eventually meet a junction with a fingerpost. Continue ↑ and follow the track as it drops over limestone to meet a tarmac lane.

4 Turn ←, crossing a cattle grid, and continue until you meet crossroads. Go ↑, and at a T-junction, bear → to ride along this tarmac lane until you meet a turning on your **right** signed *Malham Field Centre*. Take this and ride past buildings and then through a small gorge to reach the field centre.

5 Go around the **LH** side of the building and continue on the bridleway as it drops quickly to meet **Malham Tarn**. Keep on this track as it skirts the eastern shore of the tarn then bear → at the first fork (below crags) to stay on the distinct track. After passing through a gate turn → along the *Pennine Way*. Then at the corner of the drystone wall, which encircles a cluster of trees, bear ← (in effect ↑) to follow the grassy bridleway to meet a car park.

6 Turn → onto a tarmac lane, then, after passing through a gap in a wall, turn first ← onto a bridleway signed *Langscar Gate*. After around 20m, at another fingerpost, bear → towards *Langscar Gate* and follow this grassy track past limestone escarpments, through a drystone wall, and across another field to meet a tarmac lane.

7 At Langscar Gate go ← then turn immediately → onto a byway signed *Cow Close Langcliffe*. Climb the rocky path to meet a fork at a fingerpost and turn ← signed *Stockdale Lane*.

8 Follow the grassy bridleway over several fields to meet a wider track. Turn → towards Stockdale Lane and after a short distance reach the top of a long and cracking descent. Enjoy this rocky twisting delight.

9 At the bottom of the sketchy blast emerge at a tarmac lane. Turn → onto Stockdale Lane and descend to meet a T-junction. Turn → then take the first bridleway ← signed *Lambert Lane*. Follow this to emerge at another tarmac lane, turn ←, signed *Long Preston* and follow the sandy surfaced bridleway.

10 After a short distance fork → over rubble to a gated bridleway, signed *Turnpike House*. Follow this track as it descends steeply to meet a gate. Pass through and bear ← at the bottom. Ride to the **RH side of the Lodge Farm** buildings and descend the tarmac Lodge Road as it gives a fast descent all the way to meet the **B6480**. Turn → and follow this road back into **Settle**.

On the easy track around Malham Tarn

The fast walled lane descent into Stainforth

22 The Ribble Rumble

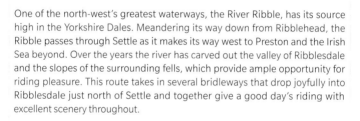

Start/Finish	Settle SD 819 637
Distance	32km (20 miles)
Off road	16km (10 miles)
On road	16km (10 miles)
Ascent	955m (3135ft)
Grade	▲
Time	3hrs 30mins–4hrs 30mins
Parking	Pay and display in Settle
Pub	The Lion, Settle; The Craven Heifer, Stainforth
Café	Settle Down Café, Settle (but bring sandwiches as well)

One of the north-west's greatest waterways, the River Ribble, has its source high in the Yorkshire Dales. Meandering its way down from Ribblehead, the Ribble passes through Settle as it makes its way west to Preston and the Irish Sea beyond. Over the years the river has carved out the valley of Ribblesdale and the slopes of the surrounding fells, which provide ample opportunity for riding pleasure. This route takes in several bridleways that drop joyfully into Ribblesdale just north of Settle and together give a good day's riding with excellent scenery throughout.

Overview

Leaving Settle, an easy spin along fairly level road to Langcliffe warms the legs for the very steep climb out of the village. Following this climb a fast and fun drop throws you into the lovely village of Stainforth – tight bends and drainage ruts are good reasons to keep a check on your speed. A lengthy tarmac climb towards the towering Pen-y-ghent is followed by a good descent down the aptly named Long Lane. An interesting climb up Moor Head Lane then leads to more tarmac climbing before opening up into a quick blast with good views over Malham Tarn. On the return leg you take in the well maintained – if somewhat sanitised – track of the waymarked Settle Loop. You drop below Langcliffe Scar and then pick up a nice bridleway that takes you steadily downwards back into the centre of Settle ready for a well-earned cup of tea.

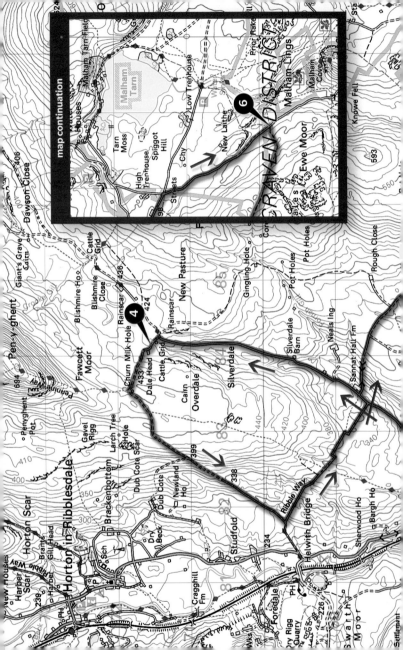

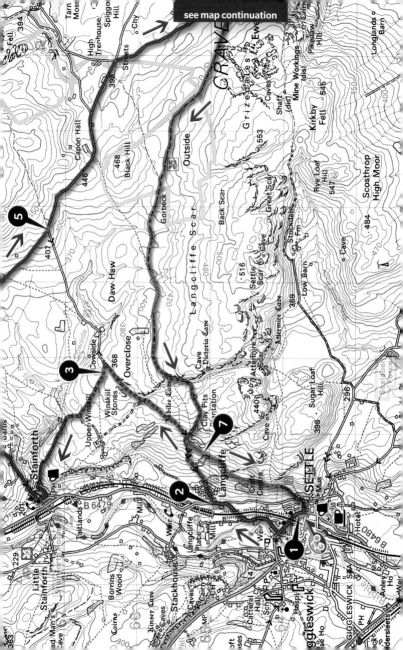

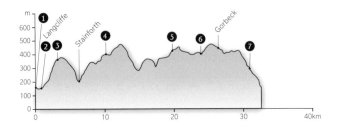

Directions

1 From the centre of **Settle**, head north towards Giggleswick. Just before the road crosses the River Ribble turn ➜ onto the `B6479` and ride to **Langcliffe**.

2 At Langcliffe turn ➜ and after passing a church climb steeply with a 20% gradient in places. After passing over a cattle grid ignore a left turning signed *Pennine Bridleway* and continue to climb ↑. Descend a short distance and turn ← (just before a second cattle grid) onto an unsigned track.

Watch your footwork on the stepping stones in Stainforth

3 Follow this trail and pass through a gate onto a walled lane. This gives a fast drop into **Stainforth** (watch for tight corners and drainage ruts). In Stainforth bear → at a green and use stepping stones to cross the beck – (if the stones are submerged

Dropping into Ribblesdale on Long Lane

follow the road and turn first →, then first → again). Turn → and climb Goat Lane. Ignore the first left turn with a byway and continue ↑ passing **Sannat Hall Farm** on your right. Descend then climb up a road to meet a ← turn by a limestone pavement signed *Pennine Way*. Take this track.

4 Follow this good, stone-surfaced trail to a fork at **Dale Head**. Bear ← towards *Helwith Bridge* and enjoy a long, fast descent down Long Lane, passing through a couple of gates to meet another fork. Turn ← and climb Moor Head Lane to meet a tarmac lane, turn ← then first → onto another tarmac road. Descend steeply then climb sharply and follow the lane to meet a T-junction.

5 Turn ← (in effect ↑). Descend at speed and at the next junction turn →, then turn → again at a crossroads near **Malham Tarn**. Follow this lane to a byway turning on the **right** just after a small lay-by (**easy to miss as obscured by a drystone wall protrusion**).

6 Take the byway and follow this track to meet a fork with a fingerpost. Turn → towards Langcliffe and follow the wide easy, undulating track (part of the waymarked *Settle Loop*) over open moorland. This trail eventually drops quickly to meet a tarmac lane. Turn sharp ← to pass through a gate and onto a bridleway signed to *Settle*.

7 Follow this bridleway, passing through several gates, as it drops steadily towards Settle – the last section is steep and watch for drainage ruts. Turn ← onto a tarmac lane and descend in the centre of **Settle**.

Passing Addlebrough on the dusty trail to Cubeck

23 Raydale

START / FINISH	Bainbridge SD 934 902
DISTANCE	33km (20½ miles)
OFF ROAD	23km (14¼ miles)
ON ROAD	10km (6¼ miles)
ASCENT	1150m (3775ft)
GRADE	▲
TIME	4hrs–5hrs
PARKING	On street in Bainbridge
PUB	Rose and Crown Hotel, Bainbridge
CAFÉ	Bring sandwiches

70%
OFF ROAD

This is a cracking route that explores a relatively little known area right in the heart of the Yorkshire Dales. Tracks that climb and descend the southern flank of Wensleydale provide interesting riding, as well as excellent wide views over this world famous dale that has become synonymous with the creamery producing delicious cheeses a few miles west.

The route's main focal point, however, is the hidden valley of Raydale. A tranquil backwater, sparsely populated and containing the picturesque Semer Water tarn, one of the national park's few bodies of water. This is a tough ride that packs in plenty of climbing and is also full of rewards, with a rich variety of great descents.

OVERVIEW

Starting from Bainbridge you climb into the mouth of Raydale before bearing off and descending the southern flank of Wensleydale. A short pedal to the characterful hamlet of Thornton Rust is swiftly followed by a climb onto and over moorland to contour around imposing Addlebrough. More climbing on an ancient drovers' track then gives way to a long high-speed blast into Raydale. After dropping to the valley floor and fording becks you climb back out of the dale, passing Semer Water and high onto the fell above. A very steep tarmac section is followed immediately by an even steeper bridleway. The gradient soon relents, though, to take you to the Cam High Road – a former Roman highway. A fantastic descent to

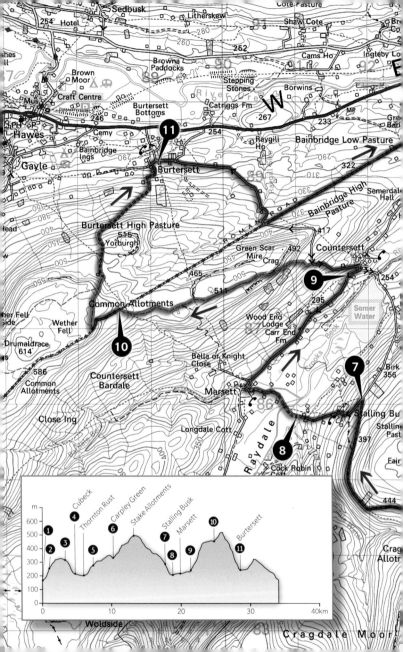

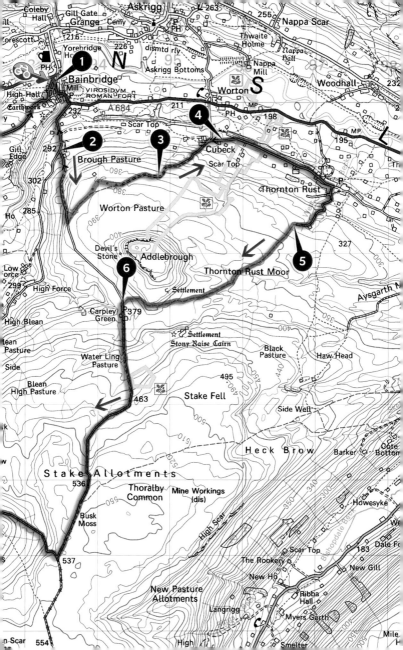

Burtersett is followed by more tarmac climbing before the blisteringly quick finale down the Cam High Road returns you to Bainbridge.

DIRECTIONS

1 Starting from **Bainbridge**, ride **SE** along the `A684` a short distance to cross the River Bain by a garage. Turn first → and climb Carpley Green Road. After another short distance turn ← at a fork beneath a radio mast, signed to *Carpley Green*.

2 Continue climbing until the track levels out, look for and take a bridleway ← to *Cubeck*. Follow this bridleway, with **Addlebrough** on your right, as it hugs the field's **left** perimeter wall. Ignore the first wall opening and follow the trail to the field's corner. Pass through a gate and continue ↑, taking either of the two paths ahead as they rejoin at the next wall.

3 Go through the gate and ride across the next field, then, at the next wall, ride through the gap and turn sharply ←. Follow the track as it gives a fine descent to the farm at **Cubeck**.

4 At the road turn → and follow it to **Thornton Rust**. Turn → opposite the Village Institute building, following a sign for *car parking*. At the small car park fork ← after a shallow ford and follow the firm track as it climbs steadily onto moorland.

5 Bear ← at the fork with a fingerpost. Enjoy good moor riding on the grassy path, passing through the first gate and continuing ↑. Keep to the main trail and pass through a gate with a stile. Continue ↑, ignoring a permissive footpath to the right, and ride to meet and pass through a gate with a bridleway sign attached. The bridleway eventually gives a short singletrack descent to emerge at **Carpley Green**.

Preparing to leave Stalling Busk

6 Turn ← and continue ↑ through the farm taking the long Busk Lane track as it climbs steadily up onto **Stake Allotments**. Keep following this wide trail to a T-junction with another byway. Turn →, signed to *Stalling Busk*, and enjoy the very long and high-speed descent to meet a tarmac lane.

The long climb up to Stake Allotments

7 Turn ← and drop into **Stalling Busk**, bearing → to meet the church. Take the track opposite the church, signed to *Marsett*, and descend this technically challenging trail to the valley floor.

8 Follow the stone and rock surfaced byway as it meanders through fords (liable to flooding after heavy rains) and across the bottom of **Raydale** to **Marsett**. Turn → onto the tarmac lane, cross the bridge over Marsett Beck and follow the road to a junction by **Countersett**, overlooking **Semer Water**.

9 Turn ← at this staggered crossroads up the road signed to *Burtersett and Hawes*. Climb very steeply until the road bends sharply to the **right**, and take the bridleway forking to the ← signed to *Wether Fell*. Climb this incredibly steep grass and rock path onto **Common Allotments** – you win full marks for riding it all. Continue ↑ and pass through several fields to eventually meet the obvious **Roman road** called the Cam High Road.

10 If your legs have gone to mush you can turn → here and descend all the way back to Bainbridge. To continue on the route, however, go **L** and head uphill for a short distance to meet a bridleway on the **right** just before the top. Pass through the gate and follow this narrow grassy bridleway as it steadily morphs into an excellent, long, fast and twisting plunge down to **Burtersett**.

11 At the tarmac lane, turn → and follow the road as it climbs steadily back up to meet a crossroads with the Cam High Road. Turn ← (signed *Byway to Bainbridge*) and enjoy the benefits of Roman engineering on this long straight plummet to another tarmac lane. Bear ← (in effect ↑) and continue descending back into **Bainbridge**.

Approaching Winterings, near Gunnerside

24 Tour of Swaledale

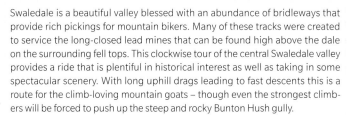

START/FINISH	Reeth SE 038 993
DISTANCE	33km (20½ miles)
OFF ROAD	26km (16¼ miles)
ON ROAD	7km (4¼ miles)
ASCENT	1270m (4165ft)
GRADE	▲
TIME	4hrs–5hrs
PARKING	On street in Reeth
PUB	The Black Bull, Reeth; King's Head, Gunnerside
CAFÉ	Dales Bike Centre, Fremington

Swaledale is a beautiful valley blessed with an abundance of bridleways that provide rich pickings for mountain bikers. Many of these tracks were created to service the long-closed lead mines that can be found high above the dale on the surrounding fell tops. This clockwise tour of the central Swaledale valley provides a ride that is plentiful in historical interest as well as taking in some spectacular scenery. With long uphill drags leading to fast descents this is a route for the climb-loving mountain goats – though even the strongest climbers will be forced to push up the steep and rocky Bunton Hush gully.

OVERVIEW

This ride is characterised by long gradual climbs on good, wide, firm tracks on open moorland providing expansive views over the Swaledale area. These climbs are then followed by very fast descents on these trails, which were created to serve the former lead mining industry from the 18th and 19th centuries. There is one short push up Bunton Hush – a gully created by mining activity – from Gunnerside Gill where the gradient is particularly steep. While overall not particularly tough technically, one descent, to Low Houses Farm, provides some food for thought, predominantly due to its very steep gradient.

see map continuation

Great
Pinseat
583

Whetshaw
Bottom

(dis)

Turf Mc

Forefield
Rake

Friarfold
Moor

Friarfold
Rake

Surrender Moss

Bouldershaw Ho

421

Mines
(dis)

Level Ho
(ruin)

550

Reeth High Moor

Moor Ho

Barras End

C K S M O O R

578

97

98

39

Mill
Bottom

Winterings
Edge

572

540

Brownsey Moor
538

520

500

Feetham Pasture

Standard

Mine Workings (dis)

530

480

347 Kearton

Winterings

Whin Hall

Brownsey
Ho

Peat Gate
Head

Potting

Barf
End

430

Blades

PH

Bents

410

Brownsey

Feetham

Dyke
Heads
Mus

Lodge Green

Heights

Low Row Pasture

390

Open Farm

S

unnerside
PH
P

Swale

Strands

330

Smarber

Low
Row

Dro

Hag Wood

Spring
End

Bank Heads

Haverdale
Ho

205

Low Ho

332

Satron Hangers

Nettlebed Ho

Robson
Ho

Hunt
Ho

Cattle
Grid

Ca

High

274

300

Crackpot

Bents
Ho

448

380

Mine Workings
(dis)

Kend
Botte

Beacon
524

Whitside
Tarn

W h i t a s i d e M o o r

565
Pickerst
Ridg

Mine Workings
(dis)

551

Aberdene Tarn

Vir
M

map continuation

North
Hush

M E L   B E C K S

Mines
(dis)

Silver
Hill

Winterings
Edge

550

500

DIRECTIONS

1 Descend from the centre of **Reeth** along the `B6270` to **Grinton**. After crossing the River Swale turn immediately → (in effect ↑) and climb through the village. Keep climbing to meet a fork on the **right** signed to *Redmire*. Take this lane, riding past bridleway turnings on both sides, to meet a **LH** bend. Turn → onto a signed bridleway forking from this bend.

2 Ride along this grassy and stony path to meet a more distinct track. Bear → (in effect ↑) and follow this good, wide track for around 6km as it climbs high then undulates above Swaledale. Keep going ↑, passing a large dark wooden building, and ignoring all turnings. Eventually you reach a T-junction by a pile of rubble. Bear → and enjoy a long, fast and twisting descent on a wide bridleway to meet a tarmac lane. Turn →.

3 After crossing a bridge over a beck turn ← onto a signed bridleway and descend next to the beck. You will need to dismount as the track narrows before meeting a gate. Pass through and follow the path over a field to a walled track. Bear → then turn ← through a gateway. Continue descending down a very steep field to emerge at a gate by **Low Houses Farm**.

4 Turn ← and follow the lane to a T-junction. Bear ← (in effect ↑) then turn → at the first junction. Follow this tarmac lane to a gate. After this the track deteriorates. Keep going as it follows the **River Swale** upstream (the track may flood after very heavy rainfall – if you suspect this to be the case then take the higher tarmac lane running parallel). Eventually when you emerge onto a tarmac lane, turn →. Then at the T-junction turn immediately → onto the `B6270` and cross the River Swale to ride into **Gunnerside**.

5 Stay on the `B6270` as it bears **right** around a bend. After passing the Penny Farthing Tearoom take the next ←, passing through an electric operated gate, to climb steeply. Ride up this long tarmac ascent to the road's end at a gate – very tough. Pass through and bear ←. Keep following this main, distinct path past cottages and along **Winterings Edge**. At a fork by a lime kiln bear ← and descend to meet an old mining building above **Gunnerside Gill**. Continue past to ride to a fingerpost. Bear → here, signed to *Surrender Bridge*, and climb the steep bridleway up the steep-sided gully of Bunton Hush – this will require considerable pushing. Continue climbing ↑ to reach the top of **Melbecks Moor**.

There are stunning vistas over Swaledale from Harkerside Moor on this fine route

6 At a large stone cairn head to a smaller cairn and bear → to pick up the wide track through mining spoils. Follow this for a short distance before it gives a fast descent over loose stones to meet a fork by a stone bridge just before a gate. Turn ← and climb the obvious path all the way to near the summit of **Great Pinseat** 583m (1913ft), ignoring all turnings. From here continue ↑ and enjoy another long and fast descent on the wide track to meet a tarmac lane. Turn ←.

7 Ride to cross a ford and climb steeply as the road bends to the **right**. As it bends back to the **left** turn → onto a signposted bridleway. Pass through a gate and ride a short distance before forking → onto a singletrack bridleway. Follow this interesting path across open land to meet a fork with a bridleway sign. Bear → and ride a short distance to a junction with a wider track. Go ↑ and continue descending.

8 Drop to meet a building at **Nova Scotia** and continue over the tarmac lane and past rocks to continue your descent on the grassy bridleway as it zig-zags steeply to meet a gate at the bottom of the field. Pass through and ride across the next field to meet a white iron gate. Pass through this and bear ←. Emerge by buildings and continue past to descend a long straight track to a junction with a tarmac lane. Turn ←, ride to another junction and bear ← again. Follow this road back into **Reeth**.

The excellent long descent of Arten Gill

25 The Cam Fell Cracker

START/FINISH	Ribblehead SD 765 793
DISTANCE	33.5km (20¾ miles)
OFF ROAD	22.5km (14 miles)
ON ROAD	11km (6¾ miles)
ASCENT	850m (2790ft)
GRADE	▲
TIME	4hrs–5hrs
PARKING	Lay-bys at Ribblehead
PUB	The Station Inn, Ribblehead
CAFÉ	Bring sandwiches

This excellent ride in the heart of the Dales contains two scintillating descents that will provide wide grins for two-wheeled adrenaline junkies. The first, a smooth fast and furious blast from the top of the Cam High Road to Newby Head Pass, is a high-speed thriller with plentiful chances to catch some air off the track's bumps. The second, a drop down Arten Gill, is a steeper and trickier affair with loose rocks and nasty drainage ruts. There are also big climbs to satisfy those who enjoy uphill challenges as well as glorious descents.

OVERVIEW

A short road spin south from Ribblehead takes you to Selside and the Pennine Bridleway. After crossing the River Ribble the long ascent of Cam Fell and the Cam High Road is made. This is followed by the splendid drop to Newby Head Pass. A short road section then leads to the day's toughest climb, a steep pull up the flank of Wold Fell. The pain is short lived, however, and is soon replaced with joy as you plummet down Arten Gill. A road climb up Dent Head then leads to a final bridleway section that gives good undulating riding before dropping back to the road leading down to Ribblehead and the starting point.

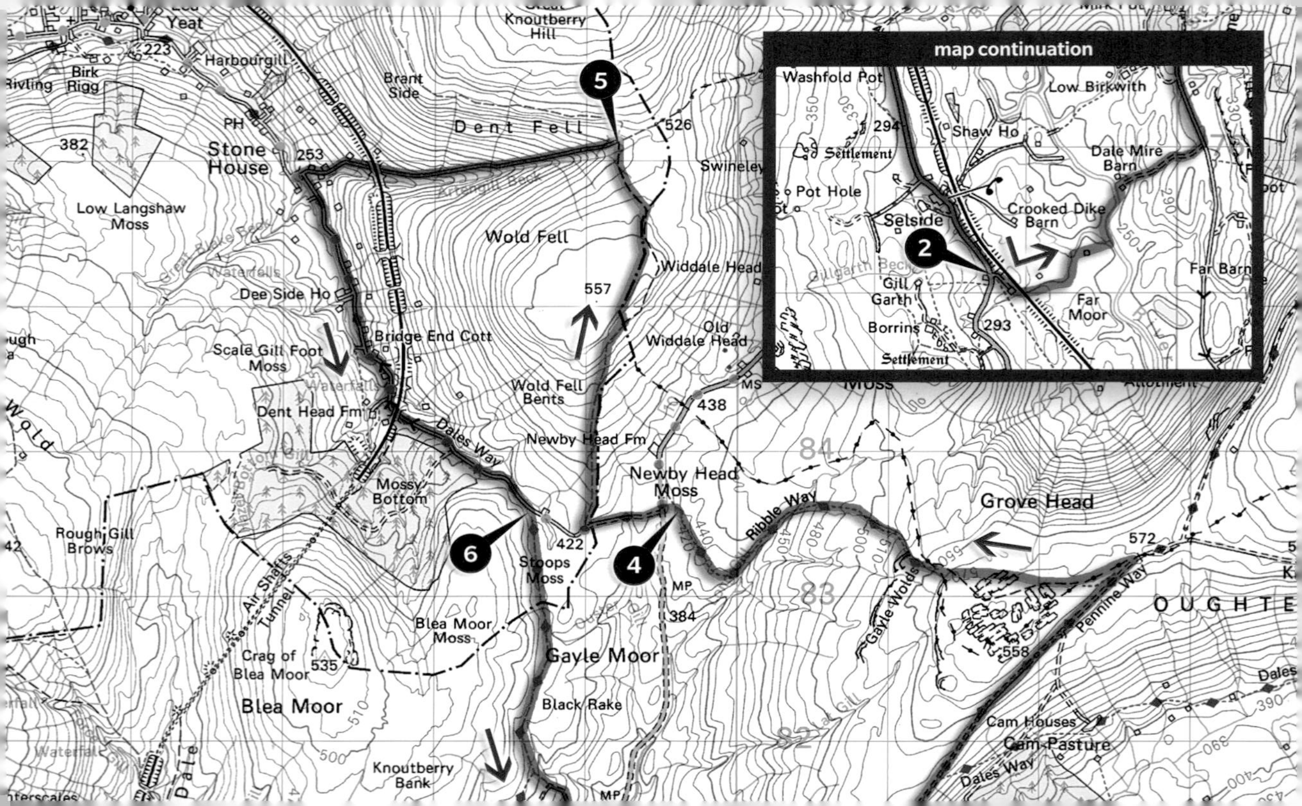

map continuation
Washfold Pot
Low Birkwith
Shaw Ho
Settlement
Pot Hole
Dale Mire Barn
Crooked Dike Barn
Selside
Gill Garth
Borrins
Far Moor
Far Barn
293
294
2
Yeat
223
Harbourgill
Birk Rigg
Knoutberry Hill
Brant Side
Dent Fell
526
5
PH
Stone House
253
382
Low Langshaw Moss
Swineley
Wold Fell
557
Widdale Head
Old Widdale Head
Dee Side Ho
Bridge End Cott
Scale Gill Foot Moss
Wold Fell Bents
Dent Head Fm
Dales Way
Newby Head Fm
438
Newby Head Moss
Ribble Way
Grove Head
572
Mossy Bottom
Rough Gill Brows
6
422
4
Stoops Moss
MP
384
Gayle Wolds
Pennine Way
558
Air Shafts
Tunnel
Blea Moor Moss
Gayle Moor
Crag of Blea Moor
535
Blea Moor
Black Rake
Cam Houses
Cam Pasture
Knoutberry Bank
84
83
82

Cam Fell Woodlands

Round Hill

CAM FELL

High Green Field

Cow Pasture

High Green

Cosh

Green Haw Moor

Birkwith Allotment

Lord's Seat

Birkwith Moor

Sike Moor

Old-Ing Moor

Cave Hill

Calf Holes

Birkwith Cave

Old Ing

Pennine Way

Cam End

Cam Houses

High Birkwith

Low Birkwith

Shaw Ho

Dales Way

Deer Bank

Ling Gill

Crutchin Gill Rigg

Browgill Cave

Nether Lodge

Selside Moss

Selside Shaw

Selside Pot

Gearstones

Far Gearstones

Cave Beck

Intack

Holme Hill

Winshaw

Dales Way

Ribble Way

Ribble Way

Thorns

Caves

Garrs

Ashes

Lodge Hall

B 6479

Stone Ho

Settlement

Washfold Pot

Ribblehead

B 6255

Runscar Scar

Cave

RIBBLEHEAD STA.

Gauber

Gauber High Pasture

Colt Park

Settlement

Park Fell

Fell Close

South House Moor

Little Dale Beck

Winterscales

Gunnerfleet

Ribblehead Viaduct

Low Sleights

Ellerbeck Pasture

Settlement

Cairn

Nether Scales Fell

Cove

1

3

see map continuation

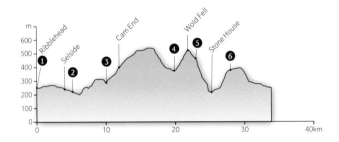

Directions

1 From the lay-bys at **Ribblehead** turn onto the `B6479` signed to *Horton in Ribblesdale* and ride until reaching the hamlet of **Selside**. Continue riding along this road out the other side of Selside until you climb a short rise. At the top of the rise turn ←, by a sign warning motorists of horses, to pass through a gate and onto a gravel-surfaced path. This is the Pennine Bridleway.

2 Descend across a field and pass under a railway bridge. Keep following the main path to meet a sturdy bridge over the River Ribble. Cross and climb the track on the far side to meet a tarmac lane and turn ←. Ride to the end of the tarmac and continue ↑ passing through a gate to follow the sign to *Cam End*. Ride to a fork and turn ← to continue following signs to Cam End.

3 Ride to pass over Ling Gill Beck and climb to a junction of trails at **Cam End**. Turn → and climb gradually up the Cam High Road, passing through a couple of gates, to eventually meet tarmac. Continue riding ↑ to reach a gate. Go through and turn immediately ← following the sign for *Newby Head Road*. Pass through a gate and ride on a distinct grassy path over undulating

Crossing the sturdy bridge over the River Ribble near Selside

Approaching Arten Gill Viaduct

ground to meet another gate. The fun begins on the other side. Enjoy this exhilarating fast drop, which twists and turns and gives plenty of opportunities for jumps.

④ At the bottom turn → on to the Newby Head Road then turn immediately ← following the sign for *Dent*. After a short distance turn → onto a trail signed to *Arten Gill Moss*. Endure a very steep climb up **Wold Fell** to a gate, go through, and continue on the now grassy tarmac as it continues to rise before dropping to meet a wide walled track. Turn ← following the sign for *Stone House*.

⑤ A cracking long plunge ensues down Arten Gill. **This is fun and fast but littered with menacing drainage ruts.** Pass under the viaduct and continue the ever steepening descent to emerge on tarmac near to **Stone House**. Continue ↑ to meet a T-junction and turn ←. Ride steadily uphill until the road steepens at **Bridge End Cottage**. Climb back under the railway and ride to the road's summit. Shortly after it levels out turn → at a gate following the sign *Bridleway to B6255*.

⑥ Follow this rocky, but interesting, bridleway called Black Rake Road as it undulates and then descends to a gate. Pass through and continue riding to emerge on tarmac by a farm. Descend the tarmac to meet the B6255 and turn →. Follow the road back to the lay-bys at **Ribblehead**.

Embarking on the excellent steep singletrack plunge off Embsay Crag

26 Embsay Crag and Flasby Fell

60% OFF ROAD

START/FINISH	Hetton SD 961 587
DISTANCE	30.5km (19 miles)
OFF ROAD	18.5km (11½ miles)
ON ROAD	12km (7½ miles)
ASCENT	850m (2790ft)
GRADE	◆
TIME	4hrs–5hrs
PARKING	On street in Hetton
PUB	The Angel Inn, Hetton
CAFÉ	Embsay station (but bring sandwiches as well)

Just north of Skipton, in the south-east corner of the Yorkshire Dales, there are a number of attractive fells and moors that contain a series of tracks that, when brought together, make a very fine mountain bike ride. Combining fast wide tracks over moorland, with singletrack climbs up and down steep rocky crags, this ride is full of variety and contains plenty of riding interest, as well as spectacular scenery. The climb and descent from Embsay Crag is a particular highlight although this very steep descent should only be undertaken by those confident in their bike-handling abilities.

OVERVIEW

A short tarmac ride from Hetton takes you to the foot of Embsay and Barden Moors. A steep climb soon has you on higher ground and provides cracking plateau riding with expansive views. A descent from Barden Moor continues at speed to Halton East before a tarmac spin and a short bridleway bring you to the toughest climb of the day. It is a steep pull up to the top of Embsay Crag, though it is entirely manageable and the gates seem to be helpfully located to provide necessary rests – award yourself a gold star if you ride all the way to the summit. Enjoy the wide views from the top before making the excellent, but very steep and tricky, descent down the flank of the crags. This descent soon widens and gives a very fast blast to Embsay Reservoir. More tarmac riding takes you to Flasby Fell and a long arduous climb – due to the grassy surface more than the gradient.

26 EMBSAY CRAG AND FLASBY FELL 181

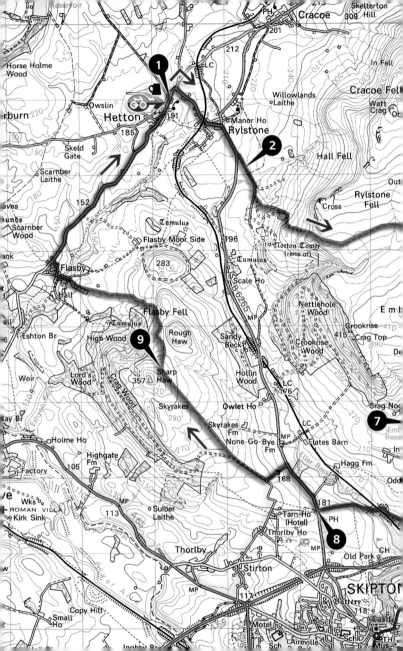

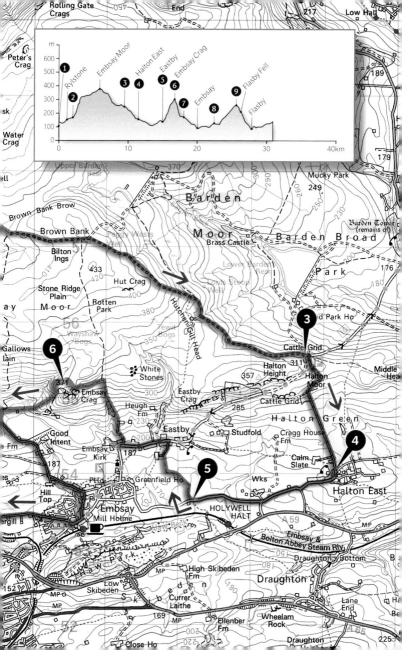

Another good descent is found on the other side, although you will have to pick your way through the occasional boggy patch.

DIRECTIONS

1 Starting in **Hetton** head **NE** towards Grassington, passing The Angel Inn on your left. Descend to the edge of Hetton and at a junction turn → and ride to **Rylstone**. At a T-junction with the `B6265` turn → and ride a short distance to meet a bridleway turning on the **left** signed *Halton Height*.

2 The next section covers around 8km. Take this stone-surfaced bridleway, ignore the first bridleway turning left and take the second ← at a gate signed *Barden Moor*. Pass through the gate and climb steeply to the next gate. Pass through and continue ↑ along the path. Continue through another gate and onto excellent singletrack. This leads you to a wider doubletrack path – bear ← onto it and follow as it climbs then descends to its culmination at a car park, ignoring all turnings.

3 Pass through the small car park and cross ↑ over the road (do not cross the cattle grid). Follow the unsigned bridleway as it descends then swings **right**. Keep to the main path as it takes you to a gate. Pass through and descend the long straight bridleway ahead to meet a tarmac lane by some buildings as you enter **Halton East**.

4 Continue ↑ to meet a T-junction and turn →. Follow this wider lane for just over 2km to meet a signed public bridleway and turn → just before a large stone barn. Keep to this stone-surfaced track, which leads to **Eastby**. At the tarmac road turn ← and ride a short distance until you see a sign *Bondcroft Farm and Bed and Breakfast*. Just before this turn → up a bridleway signed *Embsay Crag and reservoir*.

Good singletrack on Embsay Moor

5 Climb the steep tarmac bridleway to a farm then continue ↑ onto a grass surface. The track maintains a tough gradient but has a couple of gates seemingly strategically placed to allow for a breather. After the second gate continue ↑ and then follow the

Admiring the panorama from Embsay Crag

distinct path as it swings **left**. Keep to this track as it climbs very steeply to the summit of **Embsay Crag** – a tough challenge but manageable for the very fit.

6 From the top turn → (N), towards Embsay Moor, and follow the sinuous singletrack path that gives an increasingly steep descent down the flank of Embsay Crag. This excellent path passes over several large rocks before the gradient relents a little. It then widens and leads to a crossroads of tracks. Bear → and follow this superb, fast descent, to a wooden bridge. Cross and follow the main path until it meets a wider stone-surfaced track and turn ←.

7 Ride along the path to a fork and bear → onto a tarmac lane. Take this as it gives a long descent into **Embsay**. Pass the primary school and turn → at the fork by the Elm Tree pub. Stay on this road as it passes the Cavendish Arms and then turn → onto Brackenley Lane. Follow this lane to its end at a T-junction with the `B6265` and turn →.

8 Ride to the next junction and turn ←. Climb the narrow tarmac lane to a **LH** bend and turn → signed *Bridleway Flasby*. Climb the stone-surfaced track until you meet a fork with a grassy signed bridleway on the **right**. Take this and ascend the energy-sapping path to meet a small wooden bridge. Cross this and then after crossing a second bridge bear → (in effect ↑) onto a less distinct path. This is the bridleway – follow it over soft ground to meet a wooden gate.

9 Go ↑ and descend to meet another gate. Bear ← and keep to the obvious main track (ignoring all turnings), which provides an excellent long drop through several fields, interrupted by a couple of gates, several boggy patches and a small beck. After finally arriving in **Flasby**, courtesy of a final fast singletrack section, go ↑ to meet a fork and bear →. Ride to meet a T-junction and turn →. Follow this road to return to **Hetton**.

The sketchy descent into Widdale

27 A Tour West of Hawes

START/FINISH	Hawes SD 869 898
DISTANCE	42km (26 miles)
OFF ROAD	26.5km (16½ miles)
ON ROAD	15.5km (9½ miles)
ASCENT	1140m (3740ft)
GRADE	◆
TIME	4hrs 30mins–5hrs 30mins
PARKING	Pay and display in Hawes
PUB	The Moorcock Inn, near Garsdale
CAFÉ	Chaste, Hawes (but bring sandwiches as well)

Famous for its Wensleydale cheese production, Hawes is a major settlement right in the heart of the Yorkshire Dales. Its central location makes it a fine base for a biking trip and this route is a good example of the quality riding available in the vicinity of this charming market town. A ride of stiff climbs and rocky technical descents, this is a test for the more experienced riders and shows off some of the Dales' finest scenery – which looks its best on a fine, clear summer's day.

OVERVIEW

A steady road ride west out of Hawes brings you to the start of The Highway – a byway that involves a long straight and steep climb to reach its loftier sections. A bumpy descent from The High Way on the Pennine Bridleway brings you in turn to The Moorcock Inn and then Garsdale. A long tarmac climb up the Coal Road then leads to a fine bridleway that contours high around the flank of Great Knoutberry Hill. A tricky descent from here drops you to Widdale Foot and then a steady road climb back up to Newby Head Pass. Gradual off-road climbing brings you to the West Cam Road and fine high-level riding with more cracking vistas. From here an initially very rocky and technical descent soon transforms into a wide, fast and twisting blast before a final short road section completes the return plunge into Hawes.

DIRECTIONS

1 Ride along the `A683` west out of **Hawes**, passing through **Appersett**, and cross the River Ure. Continue riding westwards until reaching a turning → at Collier Holme Farm, signed *Cotterdale only*. Take this, cross a cattle grid and turn immediately ← onto a byway signed *Hell Gill*.

2 Climb this obvious and increasingly steep track to meet a gate – full marks for clearing the climb. Pass through and continue climbing until the track levels out. The trail, known as The High Way, gives good riding as it undulates along the fell side. After passing through the next gate the path soon forks. Take the **LH** option and ride to meet a gate in the wall on your **left**. Go through

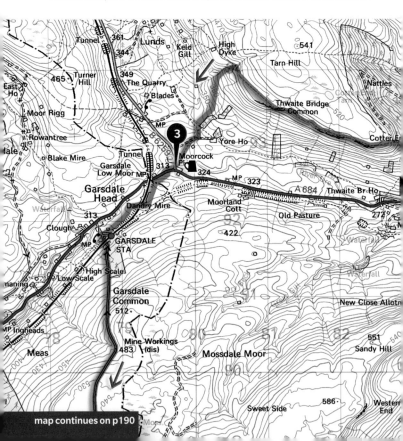

map continues on p190

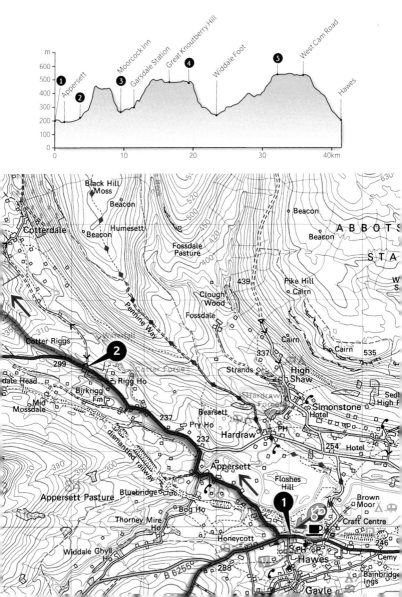

and follow the wooden posts to descend the grassy *Pennine Bridleway* and continue to drop past the trees of Cobbles Plantation. Keep to the main path as it crosses a bridge then fork ← and ride to meet the road beside the **Moorcock Inn**.

3 This section to Arten Gill covers around 8km. Cross the road and continue on the bridleway. It crosses the `A684` and passes under a railway viaduct. Keep following this track to reach **Garsdale Head**. At the road turn ← and climb past the railway station. Continue ↑ and ride up the long tarmac climb to the top. As the road descends look for an obvious turning on the **left** and take the wide bridleway, which has a drystone wall running alongside it. Follow this track as it contours around **Great Knoutberry Hill** to eventually reach a T-junction with the bridleway climbing Arten Gill. Turn ←.

4 A 14km section. After a short distance the trail begins a long, rocky and technical descent. Choose your line wisely. Eventually the path reaches a fork by a fingerpost. Bear ← following the sign to *Widdale Foot*. Ride through a sweet-smelling pine tree plantation and emerge on the `B6255` at **Widdale Foot**. Turn → and climb this road to the summit of Newby Head Pass. At a junction with the road from Dent turn ← onto a gated bridleway. Climb this

Crossing the River Ure at Appersett

Overlooking Dentdale from the flank of Great Knoutberry Hill

wide and long gravel surfaced track over moorland to emerge at a tarmac lane, passing through a gate below a crag on the way.

5 Turn ← then first ← again onto a bridleway signed *Pennine Way*. Follow this excellent track – the West Cam Road – as it gives interesting riding high above Snaizeholme. After around 3.5km the track forks. Take the ← fork, ignoring the Pennine Way option. The track, known as The Cam Road, now gives a big descent that is split into two parts. The top section is extremely technical with massive rock sections (long travel suspension is a bonus here). The second half is not as technical and gives a very fast and twisting blast to its end where it meets the `B6255`. Turn → and continue descending back into **Hawes**.

Dropping steeply from Common Allotments (Route 29)

Passing under the giant arches of Ribblehead Viaduct

28 Tour of Whernside

70% OFF ROAD

START/FINISH	Ribblehead SD 765 793
DISTANCE	39km (24¼ miles)
OFF ROAD	28km (17½ miles)
ON ROAD	11km (6¾ miles)
ASCENT	1095m (3595ft)
GRADE	▲
TIME	5hrs 30mins–6hrs
PARKING	Lay by on B6255
PUB	The Station Inn, Ribblehead
CAFÉ	Bring sandwiches

The highest of the Yorkshire Dale's three peaks, Whernside's summit is the preserve of walkers. However a fun circumnavigation of this famous fell is available for mountain bikers. This is a varied route involving tough climbs, technical rocky descents, quiet lanes, limestone pavement meanderings and moorland plateau cruising. When all these elements are pieced together with the stunning vistas on offer throughout, it provides an excellent day's riding in the southern Dales. Unusually for this book, the route does include a couple of short sections of pushing. However, persevere, as they are soon over and you are rewarded by the riding on the rest of this grand tour.

OVERVIEW

Starting from Ribblehead you pass under the arches of the famous viaduct (if you are lucky you may see a steam train passing overhead) and follow obvious bridleways to the first climb of the day. The path here has been built with walkers in mind and the steps are prohibitive to riding, so a short push ensues. Once past the steps the rest of the climb is manageable. A section of high-level riding is soon followed by an exhilarating plunge down the northern flank of Whernside into Dentdale. A steady tarmac ride up Deepdale is followed by a very steep drag up Kingsdale Head. A short descent is then followed by steeper off-road climbing by Yordas Cave and then good fellside cruising. Another technical descent on a particularly sketchy track leads to more good byways and tarmac lanes before

map continues on p200

a stiff climb up Twisleton Scars takes you to a landscape of limestone pavement. The route passes through the limestone expanses and across open moorland before steadily dropping to farm pastures. Easy bridleways are then picked up to return you at leisure to Ribblehead Viaduct.

Directions

1 From the lay-bys on the `B6255` near **Ribblehead Viaduct** ride S towards the Station Inn. Turn → onto a bridleway signed to *Gunnerfleet* and ride on to pass under the viaduct. Continue ↑, passing through a farm, and cross a beck to meet a T-junction. Turn → onto the tarmac lane and ride to another T-junction. Turn → again, following signs for *Deepdale and Whernside*, and follow the unmade track past buildings and under a railway bridge to a T-junction with another track.

2 Turn ← and follow the sign for *Dent*. Continue along this wide trail, keeping to signs towards *Deepdale*. The bridleway soon climbs steeply – a heavily built section of steps will force a dismount and a short push. Continue climbing the track ↑ ignoring the footpath forking left towards the summit of **Whernside**. Climb to a gate and

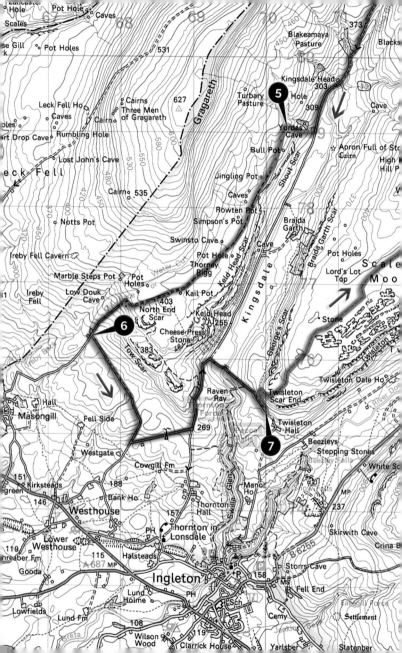

pass through. Continue ↑ on the undulating track, which gives good riding over a high plateau.

❸ The bridleway soon drops and becomes a wide walled lane. Enjoy this excellent descent, which contains very rocky technical sections, steep-sided drainage ruts and, near the bottom, a sketchy loose **LH** bend. Finally emerge onto a narrow tarmac lane and turn →. Drop to a T-junction and turn ←. Turn ← again at the next junction following signs for *Ingleton, Clapham and Settle*.

❹ This section covers around 8km. Climb gradually along this quiet tarmac lane up **Deepdale**. After crossing a beck the gradient ramps up considerably

Riding towards the famous Ribblehead Viaduct

to provide a stern test to the road's summit. From the top, descend on the road into Kingsdale, go through a gate by cottages and continue riding for just under 1km. As the road gives a short descent look for a gate on the **right** marked with an *Open Access* sign (**easy to miss**). Turn ➜ here and begin climbing the steep grassy track running to the **left** of a rocky gully, and the entrance of **Yordas Cave**, ahead.

5 Ascend the steep track, which is mostly rideable in dry conditions, to reach a gate. Pass through and bear ← to keep alongside the drystone wall. Follow to reach a gate in the corner of the field and go through. Descend the distinct track ↑ and ride to meet another gate. Continue ↑ and ride on through a paddock. **Take great care here as there are very dangerous holes running right alongside the trail.** Keep riding ↑ to pass through several more gates until a wide panorama of the **Lune valley** opens up ahead of you. This is the start of a highly rocky, loose and sketchy descent. Drop to meet a fork on the **left** by a water treatment building.

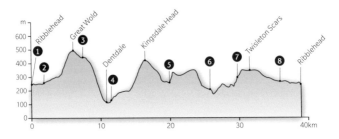

6 Turn ← and follow this track, called Tow Scar Road, as it drops to meet a T-junction with a tarmac lane. Turn ←, climb to pass a radio tower and turn ← again at the next T-junction. Descend until you see a wide unmade track on the **right** and turn here. Cross a stream and continue riding as the trail climbs briefly before running below Twisleton Scar End. Look for a bridleway turning ← and take this as it climbs steeply up the fell.

7 The track, which is rideable in the dry, zig-zags to reach high ground and meets a fork. Bear → and follow this distinct bridleway as it cuts a line through the limestone pavement above **Twisleton Scars**. The trail undulates over open moorland and passes several sections of limestone before giving a long descent to emerge at a wide stone track by a ford across a small beck.

8 Turn ← to go through a gate, following the sign to *Deepdale*. Ride through the farm at **Ellerbeck** and then on past the cottages at **Bruntscar**. Continue ↑, ignoring the road forking right, and then bear → to pass through a gate signed to *Winterscales*. Ride through several fields and through another farm to eventually reach a junction you were at near the start of the ride. Turn → here onto a narrow tarmac lane and then turn next ← to pass over a beck, through a farm, and retrace your way back under **Ribblehead Viaduct** to the starting point.

Steady climbing to the shoulder of Whernside

Overlooking Semer Water on the steep descent into Raydale

29 The Dales Leg-Breaker

START/FINISH	Horton in Ribblesdale SD 808 726
DISTANCE	58km (36 miles)
OFF ROAD	32.5km (20¼ miles)
ON ROAD	25.5km (15¾ miles)
ASCENT	1280m (4200ft)
GRADE	▲
TIME	6hrs 30mins–7hrs 30mins
PARKING	Pay and display in Horton in Ribblesdale
PUB	The Buck Inn, Buckden
CAFÉ	Buckden Village Restaurant

55% OFF ROAD

This is a big tour around the heart of the Yorkshire Dales. Including three big – but not steep – climbs and four excellent and varied descents, this route rewards those with good fitness. The riding is excellent and is only matched by the scenery. Pick a good day as you will be presented with big views from the route's high points. Other scenic highlights include passing waterfalls, one of the Dales' few significant bodies of water, Semer Water, and riverside cruising.

OVERVIEW

After riding north out of Horton in Ribblesdale, the first off-road section is reached. This track has recently been upgraded from a footpath to be incorporated into the Pennine Bridleway and gives fine riding. After crossing Ling Gill Bridge the climbing begins – a long steady ascent of the Cam High Road, an old Roman Road. From here, high level cruising is followed by a steep descent that will give a good test for your brakes. A short road section and then a rocky byway take you to the secluded hamlet of Stalling Busk. Another long gradual climb from here is followed by a fun rocky descent to a road. This is soon left behind and another bridleway picked up, which drops you pleasantly into Buckden. A long road ride alongside the River Wharf leads to the final off-road action of the day. A climb through a forest plantation leads to undulating moorland and then a long fast blast on a wide track back into Horton.

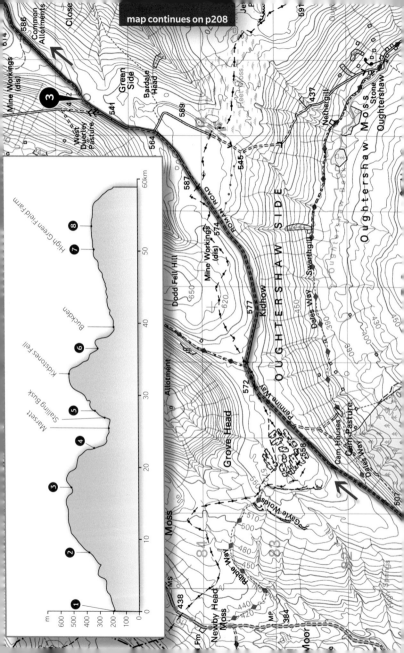

map continues on p208

Common Allotments
Close
586
614
Mine Workings (dis)
West Dukerley Pasture
541
Green Side
Baddale Head
589
Peat Moss
591
Jer...
437
Nethergill
Stone
Oughtershaw
Oughtershaw Moss
564
545
Roman Road
587
574
Dodd Fell Hill
650
620
577
Kidhow
OUGHTERSHAW SIDE
Oughtersh...
Swarthgill
450
Dales Way
390
430
400
572
Pennine Way
Cam Pasture
Cam Houses
558
Dales Way
507
Allotment
Grove Head
550
Gayle Wolds
510
500
480
Pennine Way
Ribble Way
450
440
420
384
MP
438
Newby Head Moss
Fm
Ms
Moor
Moss

High Green Field Farm
Dodd Fell Hill
Mine Workings (dis)
Buckden
Kidstones Fell
Marsett
Stallilng Busk
Allotment
Moss

m
600
500
400
300
200
100
0

0   10   20   30   40   50   60 km

① ② ③ ④ ⑤ ⑥ ⑦ ⑧

start/finish point

see inset map for start/finish

Horton in Ribblesdale

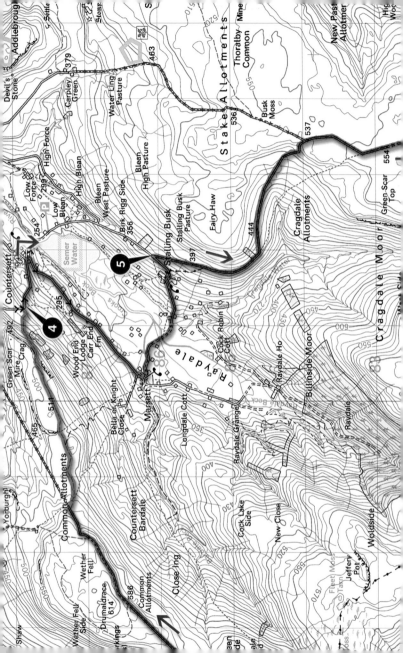

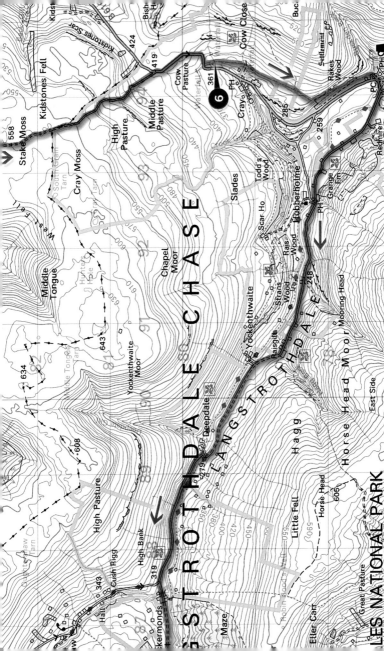

Directions

1 Starting from the pay and display car park in **Horton in Ribblesdale**, turn ← onto the `B6479`. Ride to the bridge over the **River Ribble** and just before crossing the bridge turn → onto a tarmac lane signed as a dead end. Follow the lane, initially beside the river, to its end at the farm of **High Birkwith**. Continue ↑ following the now unmade track to a fork by **Old Ing**. Turn ← and follow the wide firm-surfaced track to an old stone bridge called Ling Gill Bridge. Cross and begin climbing on the far side until reaching a T-junction and then turn → onto the Cam High Road.

2 Continue climbing steadily up the long but gradual incline to the summit of this old Roman road where it emerges onto a tarmac lane. Continue ↑, passing through several gates, to eventually meet a T-junction and turn ←. The road begins descending and just before a very steep section fork → onto a wide unmade byway.

3 After a level section the track becomes rockier and begins descending over **Common Allotments**. Look for a bridleway turning on the **right** signed to *Crag Side Road*. Take this grassy track as it descends briefly and then becomes an interesting undulating singletrack. Keep going ↑ ignoring all forks until, after passing through the fourth gate, you see the bridleway bearing **right** and downhill below a crag. Follow this steep descent with rocks and ruts that keep things lively. Go through two sets of gates and emerge on a tarmac lane.

4 Turn → and descend the road to the crossroads in **Countersett**. Turn → following the sign to *Marsett*. Follow the lane, with **Semer Water** below you, to the sleepy hamlet of **Marsett** and, after crossing a small bridge, turn ← following a rocky byway alongside Marsett Beck, signed to *Stalling Busk*. **The track has a couple of fording points and can be flooded after heavy rain so take care.** Before long it gives a technical climb up into **Stalling Busk**. Turn → opposite the church and ride out of the village.

5 This section covers around 10km. On the edge of the village, bear → onto an unmade wide byway signed to *Kidstones*. Follow this long but gradual climb to its summit and keep going ↑ at a fork, following another sign to Kidstones. After a high plateau section the track provides an enjoyable twisting and rocky descent to a road. Turn → and descend a short distance. On a sharp **LH** bend look for a bridleway turning **left**, signed to *Buckden*, and turn here.

6 Follow the distinct grassy bridleway as it gives level riding across several fields before transforming into a cracking fast blast under trees into **Buckden**. At the road at the bottom turn ← and then turn first → signed to *Hubberholme*. Ride along this tarmac road as it gradually climbs alongside the beautiful River Wharfe for around 7.5km to meet a fork at **Beckermonds**. Turn ← here, signed to *Greenfield*, and ride for a further 5km to reach **High Green Field Farm** at the end of the tarmac lane.

7 Continue ↑ onto the forest road as it continues climbing at a slight gradient through a conifer plantation. At a fork bear ← to continue along the bridleway. Ignore all turnings until reaching the edge of the forest and a choice of gates. Take the **LH** gate and follow the bridleway out of the trees and onto **Birkwith Moor**. Follow this fine undulating track to a junction with the Pennine Way. Continue ↑ to keep following the main path **S** following the sign to *Horton in Ribblesdale*.

8 The continually undulating trail provides interesting riding in a southerly direction for several kilometres until eventually pointing downwards and giving a thrilling finale by plunging you at speed back into **Horton in Ribblesdale**. At the road turn ← to cross the narrow bridge and return to your starting point.

Riding past a waterfall above Buckden

Enjoying the amazing stretch of singletrack in Bowderdale

30 The Howgills Classic

START/FINISH	Sedbergh SD 657 919
DISTANCE	38.25km (23¾ miles)
OFF ROAD	26.5km (16½ miles)
ON ROAD	11.5km (7¼ miles)
ASCENT	1260m (4135ft)
GRADE	◆
TIME	5hrs 30mins–6hrs 30mins
PARKING	Pay and display in Sedbergh
PUB	The Black Swan, Ravenstonedale
CAFÉ	The Howgills Bakery and Tea Room, Sedbergh (but bring sandwiches as well)

70% OFF ROAD

Sandwiched between the Lake District and the Dales, the Howgills are a group of fells that stand imperiously north of Sedbergh. This route provides a tour of these fells on a loop that makes for arguably one of the best days out on a bike in the UK. There is something for all experienced riders to enjoy here – high level riding with magnificent wide vistas; scintillating stretches of singletrack through deserted mountain valleys; twisting technical fun in the woods and challenging climbs for the mountain goats. Do this route once and you will want to revisit it time and time again.

OVERVIEW

Starting from the centre of Sedbergh, a short spin on a quiet tarmac lane doesn't quite prepare the legs for the stiff climb from Lockbank Farm to the ridge between Winder and Arant Haw. Enjoy the wide views of the Lakeland fells, Morecambe Bay and the nearby Dales (on a clear day) as you make your way north along the high ridge to the summit of The Calf, the highest point of the Howgills at 676m (2218ft). A right turn here and you are soon descending into Bowderdale on one of the best stretches of singletrack anywhere. This amazing trail takes you all the way to the head of the valley, after which a mix of quiet lanes and bridleways takes you into Ravenstonedale and a potential pub stop. From here, height is regained on the lane towards Adamthwaite. However, before reaching the remote farm you

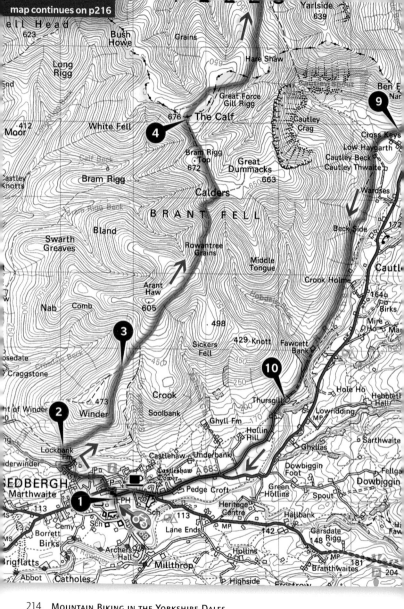

will turn off and enjoy a series of descents that culminates in a joyous weave through the trees at Murthwaite Park. The homeward leg back to Sedbergh consists of excellent bridleway riding, with more fun sections of singletrack, and passing the spectacular Cautley Spout waterfall.

Directions

1 Turn → out of the pay and display car park in **Sedbergh**. Go ↑ at the mini roundabout and follow the road as it bears **left**. Turn first → onto a narrow lane and climb in the direction of Winder. Follow this lane as it swings **left** past a children's play area and then houses. At a sharp **LH** bend turn → by **Lockbank Farm** following the sign *BW to Fell*.

2 Pass through the farm, going through two gates, still following signs for BW to Fell. The bridleway climbs steeply away from the farm to meet another gate. Go through and bear ←. Almost immediately an unlikely singletrack path climbs steeply to the **right**. Take this – a short stint of pushing will be required until the track becomes wider and swings round to the **right**. Although the track is still very steep it is now rideable all the way to the top. Keep following the track as it contours around the southern flank of **Winder** and emerges on a plateau to join a wider path just below the summit.

It's a stiff climb up to Calders

③ Turn ➜ onto this path and head **N**. Climb to meet a fork and bear ➜ following the sign *bridleway to The Calf*. The track continues to climb to the **right** of **Arant Haw** summit before levelling out and then giving a short but fun descent on a rocky trail to the foot of a steep climb up **Calders**. A push is likely to be required up part of this very steep section, however it does not last long. At the top the path dips slightly before rising to meet the summit cairn of **The Calf**.

④ Bear ➜ here, passing a small tarn on your **right**. After a short flat section the track passes another small pool, this time on the **left**. Then the track immediately plunges downwards to begin the sublime descent into Bowderdale. Steep at first, the trail is a narrow singletrack littered with ruts, drops and rocks – line choice is key here. Eventually the gradient eases but the singletrack path remains fun and interesting as it clings to the steep-sided fell above Bowderdale Beck. Follow this excellent trail all the way to the mouth of the valley (there are no forks) to meet a gate. Pass through, descend across a field to another gate, and then ride on an obvious stone-surfaced track to emerge at a tarmac lane at **Bowderdale**.

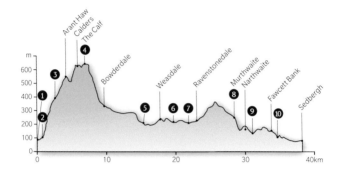

5 Turn ➜ and follow this lane to pass over a cattle grid. Turn next ➜ and then next ➜ again to ride to a fork of two bridleways by a farm. Bear ➜ (in effect ↑) and pass through a gate into the field beyond. Ride along the **RH** side of the field to the far end and pass through a gate to stay on the bridleway. Keep to the obvious path to go through another gate. Shortly after this the path meets a wider track. Bear ← and ride to Cow Bank where the track turns into a tarmac lane. Descend sharply and cross a bridge (caution, the gate may be closed on the far side), then bear ➜ at a fork by cottages at **Weasdale**. Ride along the tarmac lane, ignoring two turnings on the left, until the road meets a **RH** turning as it bends sharply **left**. Turn ➜ here (in effect ↑) and ride to meet a gate under a tree by a fingerpost.

6 Turn ➜ to pass through the gate, following the sign for *Low Greenside*. Keep to the bridleway by passing through a second gate and then passing a stone barn. Ignore the footpath forking right and climb ↑ to the gate on the brow before you. Pass through and cross ↑ over the next field. Keep following the bridleway as it becomes a narrow grassy walled track that leads to a tarmac lane. Turn ← here then first ➜. Ride to cross a bridge over a beck and then turn first ➜ by the Kings Head pub in **Ravenstonedale**.

7 Ride to meet a T-junction and bear ➜. Follow the lane as it swings **right** by the Black Swan pub and rises steadily through the centre of Ravenstonedale. Just before leaving the far end of the village turn ➜ onto a lane signed to *Artlegarth and Adamthwaite*. Keep riding towards Adamthwaite, ignoring a turning to Artlegarth. The road climbs steadily until reaching a short section of switchbacks where the gradient steepens. The road's summit is reached shortly after these bends and then it begins descending. Look for a bridleway turning on the **left** signed *Public Bridleway Murthwaite*. Take this and enjoy an undulating and increasingly rocky descent. At a junction bear ➔ and ride to meet a gate at **Murthwaite**.

8 Pass through and turn immediately ➔ following a sign for *Narthwaite*. Go through another gate and begin descending the **LH** side of the field ahead. After a short while the trail forks. Bear ➔ to drop down the centre of the field until reaching trees. Follow the trail as it becomes a snaking singletrack blast weaving its way through the woods. Eventually it spits you out into a stream that must be forded to pass into the field beyond. Ride to meet a wide track and bear ➔ to climb to the farm at **Narthwaite**. Turn ⬅ in the farm, passing through gates, and descend a rocky track, which swings to the **right**, to another gate. Keep going down this trail as it drops to another ford. Cross the stream and pick up the trail to ride a short level section and then descend on a track littered with drainage ruts.

9 At the bottom the trail swings **right** to face **Cautley Spout** waterfall. Bear ⬅ here to cross the wooden bridge and follow the bridleway ahead. Keep following the obvious narrow singletrack path as it hugs the fellside. After crossing a very small bridge bear ➔ to continue along the path as it climbs the fell slightly. Keep to this main path as it undulates through several more fields to eventually emerge by buildings at **Fawcett Bank**. The track now becomes wider and gives good riding before becoming a tarmac surface.

10 Descend this lane to meet the `A683` and turn ➔. Follow this road to retrace your way back into **Sedbergh**. Turn ⬅ at the mini roundabout to find the car park.

Riding high in the Howgills

Appendix

Bike shops in the region

From time to time you may need to pick up spare parts, stock up on energy products or get some new clothing. There are several bike shops in and around the Yorkshire Dales to cater for these needs. These include:

North Dales

Kirkby Stephen Cycle Centre
Station Yard,
Kirkby Stephen CA17 4LA
017683 71658

Leyburn Bike Repairs
Hill Top Farm, Moor Road
Leyburn DL8 5DJ
01969 623656
www.leyburnbikes.co.uk

Arthur Caygill Cycles
Borough Road
Gallowfields Trading Estate
Richmond DL10 4SX
01748 825469
www.arthurcaygillcycles.co.uk

The Dales Bike Centre
Parks Barn, Fremington
Near Reeth DL11 6AW
01748 884908
www.dalesbikecentre.co.uk

South Dales

3 Peaks Cycles
24 Market Place
Settle BD24 9EJ
01729 824232
www.3peakscycles.com

Escape Bike Shop
Kirkstead Farm, Westhouse
Ingleton LA6 3NJ
015242 41226
www.escapebikeshop.com

Outdoor Human
Unit B, Wood Lane
Grassington BD23 5LU
0845 680 0691
www.outdoorhuman.co.uk

The Bicycle Shop
3/5 Water Street
Skipton BD23 1PQ
01756 794386
www.bicycleshop.co.uk

Aire Valley Cycles
Millennium House, 74 South Street
Keighley BD21 1DQ
01535 610839
www.airevalleycycles.com

JD Cycles
The Yard, 42a Nelson Road
Ilkley LS29 8HN
01943 816101
www.jdcycles.co.uk

Listing of Cicerone Guides

For full information on all our
guides, and to order books and
eBooks, visit our website:
www.cicerone.co.uk

Walking – Trekking – Mountaineering – Climbing – Cycling

Over 40 years, Cicerone have built up an outstanding collection of 300 guides, inspiring all sorts of amazing adventures.

Every guide comes from extensive exploration and research by our expert authors, all with a passion for their subjects. They are frequently praised, endorsed and used by clubs, instructors and outdoor organisations.

All our titles can now be bought as **e-books** and many as iPad and Kindle files and we will continue to make all our guides available for these and many other devices.

Our website shows any **new information** we've received since a book was published. Please do let us know if you find anything has changed, so that we can pass on the latest details. On our **website** you'll also find some great ideas and lots of information, including sample chapters, contents lists, reviews, articles and a photo gallery.

It's easy to keep in touch with what's going on at Cicerone, by getting our monthly **free e-newsletter**, which is full of offers, competitions, up-to-date information and topical articles. You can subscribe on our home page and also follow us on **Facebook** and **Twitter**, as well as our **blog**.

Cicerone – the very best guides for exploring the world.

CICERONE

2 Police Square Milnthorpe Cumbria LA7 7PY
Tel: 015395 62069 info@cicerone.co.uk
www.cicerone.co.uk